III

Heal Thyself

Joel James Shuman

Keith G. Meador

Heal Thyself

SPIRITUALITY,

MEDICINE,

AND THE

DISTORTION

OF CHRISTIANITY

OXFORD

UNIVERSITY PRESS

2003

OXFORD
UNIVERSITY PRESS

Oxford   New York
Auckland   Bangkok   Buenos Aires   Cape Town   Chennai
Dar es Salaam   Delhi   Hong Kong   Istanbul   Karachi   Kolkata
Kuala Lumpur   Madrid   Melbourne   Mexico City   Mumbai   Nairobi
São Paulo   Shanghai   Taipei   Tokyo   Toronto

Copyright © 2003 by Oxford University Press, Inc.

Published by Oxford University Press, Inc.
198 Madison Avenue, New York, New York, 10016

www.oup.com

Oxford is a registered trademark of Oxford University Press

Library of Congress Cataloging-in-Publication Data
Shuman, Joel James.
Heal thyself : spirituality, medicine, and the distortion of Christianity / Joel James
Shuman and Keith G. Meador.
    p. cm.
Includes bibliographical references and index.
ISBN 0-19-515469-X
1. Medicine—Religious aspects—Christianity—History of doctrines. I. Meador, Keith
G. II. Title.
BT732 .S48 2002
261.5'61—dc21   2002016937

9 8 7 6 5 4 3 2 1
Printed in the United States of America
on acid-free paper

|||

Acknowledgments

This book began three years ago as a conversation between two friends who believed that Christian theology had some interesting and important things to say about sickness and health. As our work has taken shape, our friendship has deepened, and the circle of friends participating in this book's creation and development has expanded. These friends' many forms of contributing to the book's writing have made it significantly better than it could otherwise have been. We owe them a debt of gratitude for whatever good this book does. Regrettably, we cannot name them all here, and we ask in advance for the forgiveness of anyone we inadvertently exclude.

Earlier forms of the arguments offered in these pages were tested and refined in conversation with some of the best students either of us has been privileged to teach in a seminar in theology and medicine at Duke Divinity School, which we conducted together in the spring of 2001. Physicians, medical students, and seminarians sat with us every week for an entire semester and struggled to help us describe a faithful Christian engagement with the problems of illness, suffering, and death. In particular, we are grateful for the help of Tom Patamia, Fabian Kleisch, Geraldine Haywood, Todd Oswald, Warren Kinghorn, and Julia Alliger. We also want to express appreciation for conversations with Abraham Nussbaum, David Cloutier, Alex Sider, Peter Dula, and Scott Williams during the development of these ideas.

Cynthia Burris, whose theological thinking about sickness and suffering is absolutely profound, was a tremendous help to us as we developed our arguments. We hope that her work is soon published and receives the attention it deserves. Our friend Brian Volck, a talented, hardworking physician and a wonderful poet—not to mention a pretty good theologian—read and commented helpfully on an earlier version of the entire book. We regard the enthusiastic endorsement of a theologically serious Christian layperson and working physician—especially one with Brian's literary sensibilities—as a kind of litmus test for the book. Stanley Hauerwas, in addition to generously agreeing to write the foreword, also read the entire manuscript and made helpful comments on all of the chapters.

Quite apart from being a good friend, his influence on us is so significant that we dare not even begin to describe it.

The substance of chapter 1 was presented in lecture form as part of the "Perspectives" series sponsored by the Department of Medical Humanities in the Brody School of Medicine at East Carolina University. The questions raised by that audience pointed out some of the difficulties with our argument and helped us refine and clarify it. The members of the Department of Philosophy at East Carolina University engaged Joel Shuman in a rigorous conversation about questions concerning the intersection of chapters 1 and 2. And we certainly appreciate the opportunity to present part of chapter 5 at Saint Vincent's Comprehensive Cancer Center in New York as part of their extraordinary series "Spirituality, Religious Wisdom, and the Care of the Patient." Several members of that audience asked wonderful questions, and we especially appreciate the comments of Alan Astrow, Daniel Sulmasy, and Gina Garvin. We are also grateful that we had the opportunity to present parts of chapter 5 within the Caring Communities Program sponsored by The Duke Endowment in Charlotte, North Carolina.

The sheer mechanics of producing a book is a task too great for any two people, and we are thankful for the help we have had in that direction, as well. Colleagues at King's College and at Duke University have been unwavering in their support. Joan Francis, Julie Elliot, and Jason McKinney helped us obtain permission to excerpt material from other works. We are grateful to them and to the authors and publishers from whose work we learned so much. Jessie Shuman prepared the bibliography. Our editors at Oxford University Press—Cynthia Read, Theo Calderara, and Robin Miura—did a wonderful job of encouraging us and shepherding our work from prospectus to manuscript to finished product.

Finally, we offer sincere thanks to our families, who have graciously tolerated our immersion in this project and the frequent absences from them entailed by its completion. We love you all.

Lent, 2002

JOEL JAMES SHUMAN

KEITH G. MEADOR

Thanks to the following for permission to reproduce their material:

Excerpts from *Church Dogmatics*, Volume 2. Pt. 2., by Karl Barth. G. W. Bromiley and T. F. Torrance, editors. Copyright © T. and T. Clark, Edinburgh, 1957.

Excerpts from *Church Domatics*, Volume 3. Pt. 4., by Karl Barth. G. W. Bromiley and T. F. Torrance, editors. Copyright © T. and T. Clark, Edinburgh, 1961.

Excerpts from the "Ascetical Works of St. Basil the Great," found in *Fathers of the Church*, Vol. 9, Copyright © Catholic University of America Press, Washington.

Excerpts from *Fidelity: Five Stories* by Wendell Berry, copyright © 1992 by Wendell Berry. Used by Permission of Pantheon Books, a division of Random House, Inc.

Excerpts from *A Place on Earth* by Wendell Berry, copyright © 2001 by Wendell Berry. Reprinted by permission of Counterpoint Press, a member of Persens Books, L.L.C.

Reprinted from *The Wages of Goodness: Poems*, by Michael Blumenthal, by permission of the University of Missouri Press. Copyright © 1992 by Michael Blumenthal.

Excerpts form *At the Origins of Modern Atheism* by Michael Buckley. Copyright © 1987 by Yale University Press.

Hayden Carruth, "Crucifixion" (excerpt) from *Collected Shorter Poems 1946–1991*. Copyright © 1991, 1992 by Hayden Carruth. Reprinted with the permission of Copper Canyon Press, P.O. Box 271, Port Townsend, WA 98368-0271.

Excerpts from *Lectures on the Essence of Christianity*, by Ludwig Feuerbach and translated by Ralph Manheim. English translation copyright © 1967 by Ralph Manheim. Reprinted by permission of HarperCollins Publishers Inc.

Excerpts from "The Porcelain Couple" and "The Ship Pounding," from *Without* by Donald Hall. Copyright © 1998 by Donald Hall. Reprinted by permission of Houghton Mifflin Company. All rights reserved.

Excerpt from *The Beginning and the End of Religion*, by Nicholas Lash. Copyright © 1996 by Cambridge University Press. Reprinted with the permission of Cambridge University Press and the author.

Excerpts from *On Religion: Speeches to its Cultured Despisers*, by Friedrich Schleiermacher. Copyright © by Harper & Row, Publishers, Inc. Copyright © renewed 1986 by Harper and Row, Publishers, Inc. Reprinted by permission of HarperCollins Publishers Inc.

Excerpts from *The Christian Faith*, by Friedrich Schleiermacher. Copyright © by T & T Clark, Edinburgh, 1989.

Contents

Foreword

God sometimes comes up when we get sick. But the god that makes his or her appearance during times of illness often has little in common with the Trinitarian God Christians worship. This is as true for Christians as it is for those who are not Christian. For Christians, however, that the god to whom we pray when we are sick is not the God we worship creates a peculiar difficulty. That Christians confuse the god to whom we pray when we are sick with the God of Jesus Christ makes it almost impossible for us to notice we have become idolaters.

To be accused of idolatry, particularly when we are sick, seems nothing less than cruel. Being sick is usually challenging enough. To be told that when we are sick we are particularly vulnerable to sin is to quite literally rub salt in the wound. So let me explain by calling attention to a typical visit by a minister to a member of his or her congregation who is in the hospital. The minister rightly seeks to comfort by praying. They pray that god guide the hand of the surgeon and, whether the medical procedure is successful or not, that we recognize that the outcome is in god's hands.

Such prayers are no doubt sincere, but that does not make them Christian. For notice that the god to whom such prayers are directed has little to do with the God of Israel and Jesus Christ. The God of Israel and Jesus Christ is not some ultimate source of generalized compassion always ready to sympathize with us, but the God of judgment on sin and, in particular, our sin. Through the centuries the church has not let us forget, as Shuman and Meador make clear, that our sickness—and the death our being sick beacons—may well be a sign of God's judgment. We recoil from such a suggestion, desiring to protect the god to whom we pray from what can only appear to us as sadistic.

Yet the attempt to protect God (and ourselves in the process) means the god that usually is prayed to during times of illness is not worthy of worship. For that god is quite simply the god of the gaps. Such a god, the god of the gaps, was the only way many thought we could make sense of God after Newton's mechanistic physics. God simply came to name what we could not explain once it was assumed that Newton had explained the way the world works. Newton's physics has died the death of countless qualifications, but the only god that seemed possible after Newton has become the god that appears at the hospital bedside, that is, the god that takes care of anything that is beyond the power of medicine to cure.

Which means the cover of this book should be embossed with a warning that reads, "This book will not only challenge your understanding of the relation of religion and medicine, but if *Heal Thyself* is taken seriously, your life may well be disrupted." Indeed if it were possible I think those considering reading this book would be advised to sign an informed consent form. To read the book is not quite the same as participating in a clinical or experimental trial, but the results could be even more dramatic. The problem, of course, is that to be informed about the risk involved in reading the book, you need to first read the book.

Let there be no mistake, however, the position taken in this book radically challenges what most of us assume to be a given about medicine and theology. This is not another book about medical ethics but a book that changes how medical ethics should be done. This is not a book about the relation of theology and medicine, but one that challenges the politics that creates the "and" between theology and medicine. Rather than being about theology or medicine or the relation between theology and medicine, this book offers us a theological reading of the political and economic practices that produce the distorted character of current medicine and theology. Shuman and Meador do nothing less than help us discern why the god to whom we too often pray cannot help but be a god at the service of our fear of death—a fear that unfortunately shapes a medicine determined by the Promethean project to get us out of life alive.

We have long needed a book like *Heal Thyself*, and it is interesting to ask why it has not been written. At least one of the reasons is that to write a book like this is such a daunting task. Theologians seldom know enough about medicine to write a book like this, and physicians, even if they are Christians, seldom know enough about theology. That is why it is so important that this book is jointly authored by a doctor with theological training and a theologian with training in the care of the body (physical therapy). Keith Meador and Joel Shuman have joined forces not only to write a book that helps us understand the power medicine exercises in modern society and the effect that power has on our lives as Christians but also to make an argument in this book with implications that reach far beyond medical care.

The readership of this book hopefully will not be confined only to those who find their lives caught between medicine and their religious convictions. This is a book that powerfully exposes our lives to truthful analysis. By helping us see how the modern construction of "religion" is paralleled by developments in medicine, the work forces us to recognize how the loss of our fundamental ties to one another has made us sick. Yet this is a hopeful book: for the ability of the authors to diagnose so tellingly our pathologies is the result of their clarity, a clarity that is only possible through the discipline of the church, wherein lies our health. We should not be surprised, therefore, that *Heal Thyself* is a call for the rediscovery of friendship with God, one another, and even with ourselves. What a marvelous book this is that helps us rediscover the significance of the prosaic but profound truth that our health and salvation depends on what we share in common.

STANLEY HAUERWAS

III

Heal Thyself

|||

Introduction

With Eager Longing

I consider that the sufferings of the present time are not worth comparing with the glory about to be revealed to us. For the creation waits with eager longing for the revealing of the children of God; for the creation was subjected to futility, not of its own will but by the will of the one who subjected it, in hope that the creation itself will be set free from its bondage to decay and will obtain the freedom of the glory of the children of God. We know that the whole creation has been groaning in labor pains until now; and not only the creation, but we ourselves, who have the first fruits of the Spirit, groan inwardly while we wait for adoption, the redemption of our bodies.

ROMANS 8:18–19

It is a very dangerous inversion to advocate Christianity, not because it is true, but because it might be beneficial.

T. S. ELIOT

Life is hard, and never more so than when our bodies fail us and we become ill. We despise and fear illness, not only because it makes us feel bad and keeps us from doing the things we like but also because, although we know in this or that instance of being sick we probably will eventually recover, our every illness is a reminder that we are destined finally to die. And in this culture, where death is a stranger and so seems especially onerous, that is a reminder we would just as soon do without.[1]

In sickness, especially, we sense not only that things are not as we wish they were but that they are not as they should be. Illness and death confront us not simply as inconveniences but as "natural" enemies. We possess, to borrow an expression from the New Testament, an "eager longing" for life without them. Something in us suggests that the world in which we live, for all its wonder, is most certainly not the best of all possible worlds.

Learning to negotiate this seemingly ineliminable difference—between life and the world as they are and life and the world as we imagine they could or should be—is a matter close to the center of many of those ancient historical traditions we have come to call religions. This is certainly the case in the Christian tradition, where the longing for a better life and a more perfect world properly take the form of a concrete anticipation that life and the world someday will be better. Christian longing is properly not *just* longing: it is a longing and a striving thoroughly shaped by the hopeful expectation that the perfection of creation that Christians believe was accomplished in the life, death, and resurrection of Jesus of Nazareth will in God's good time be brought to completion and made real in each human life.

This is how the apostle Paul, the author of much of the New Testament, put the matter as he wrote to encourage a persecuted, suffering church in first-century Rome. The members of that community, like so many members of the Christian enclaves of the first century, doubtlessly were not simply suffering, but also were frustrated by their suffering. They longed for that deliverance promised by the Gospel they had believed. Like us, they probably wondered whether there might be something they could do to obtain it. Paul's response acknowledged and embraced the full depth of their experience of suffering and the seriousness of their longing. But he also very plainly told his fellow Christians not to expect the immediate fulfillment of all their longing. They could, if they were to remain faithful to their baptism, neither escape nor avoid suffering; it was an inevitable part of their living, not simply as persecuted Christians in a jealous Roman empire but also as broken creatures in a broken world. Yet, he admonished, this inevitability was no cause for despair, for "the sufferings of the present time are not worth comparing with the glory about to be revealed to us." That glory, he explained, encompassed the hope that the entire creation would finally "be set free from its bondage to decay" and be made perfect. In the interim, however, the apostle reminded his readers that the creation was destined to "groan inwardly while we wait for adoption, the redemption of our bodies."[2]

It is especially interesting to read Paul's word to the Christians in Rome in light of our contemporary attitudes toward our unfulfilled longing. Ours is a culture of unprecedented—some would say hubristic—striving to fulfill our longing by every means available. On the whole, humanity longs as much as ever to be delivered from illness, suffering, and death. We literally (and sometimes frantically) groan in anticipation of that deliverance. But we do not only groan in anticipation; we also struggle to deliver ourselves, less willing than generations past to tarry with our longing and more confident than they that we should not have to. Just so, we are faced with a fundamental moral question. Given the undeniable, persistent presence of an eager longing for things to be other than they are—a longing, that is, for *fulfillment*—how should Christians live in the meantime? Must Christians remain passive? Does Christian faithfulness require that we simply *wait*, or may we use the considerable resources at our disposal to recreate our lives, to make them other than they are?

|||

Religion and Medicine: A Contemporary Rapprochement

A recent proliferation of scholarly and popular literature suggests that where our longing for physical health is concerned, religious people need *not* wait—at least not as long or as often as they may once have thought. Our longing for health, suggest the authors of this literature, *can* in large part be fulfilled now, and religious faith as well as medical science can and should play a central role in that fulfillment. Professionals within and around the practice of medicine have begun to ask whether religion might be a useful adjunct to traditional scientific medicine's pursuit of good health. Beginning variously from skepticism, curiosity, casual observation, and even their own personal religious convictions, practitioners and social scientists have begun conducting controlled studies designed to examine whether there is a positive correlation between religious belief and practice—ranging from attending religious services to regular prayer and devotion to meditation to simply possessing a generally religious outlook—and good physical or mental health.[3] Generally, albeit not unequivocally, these studies suggest that such a correlation indeed does exist.[4] And recently, a number of popular books have appeared—some written by the same researchers, who are ostensibly reasoning inductively from their own prior work or the work of their peers—that commend the practice of religion, in large part because of its alleged salutary effects on physical and mental health.[5]

Surprisingly little has been written in the way of philosophical or theological critique addressing those contemporary authors who associate religious faith and practice with good mental and physical health. Our intention in this book is to do just that, to assess theologically what we frequently refer to here (as much for the sake of convenience as for descriptive accuracy) as the "contemporary rapprochement" between medicine and religion. As theologians and practitioners, we believe that there is much to be commended about the rediscovery of religious faith by scientific medicine, but we remain suspicious of the shape taken by that discovery to this point.

Our central assertion in this book is a simple one: In spite of what empirical studies show about the correlation between religion and health, it is from the perspective of faithful Christian discipleship fundamentally wrongheaded to suggest—as our colleagues sometimes seem to do—that religious belief or behavior are in some sense the efficient *cause* of better health.[6] The religiosity of the contemporary rapprochement, as interesting and worthy of ongoing consideration as it may be, is not identical to and is in many ways incompatible with what the Christian tradition has taught about sickness, health, and healing. The movement in contemporary North American culture for a more religious medicine has more to do with the fact that both religion and medicine have become phenomena shaped by the consumerist ethos of late modernity than with their traditional mutual concern for compassionate service to the sick and suffering. Religion and medicine are, in contemporary North American culture, means of achieving desirable goods external to their practice; both are increasingly viewed as means for self-interested individuals to attain the nearly universally desirable commodity that is individual health. Health is thus not simply distorted by being separated from its properly communal context; it is also, to borrow the language of Marxist critique, fetishized, meaning it is valued, pursued, and exchanged without reference to the persons or communities who produce it or to its proper place in a hierarchy of the goods of a society committed to pursuing a substantive account of human flourishing.

Consequently, we hold that just to the extent that the claims of the contemporary rapprochement are theologically uncritical, they are also susceptible to captivity by those cultural forces of late modernity that are from the perspective of historical Christianity decidedly malignant. Christianity possesses a rich tradition of praying for the sick to be healed, and a still richer tradition of caring for and being in solidarity with them. The contemporary rapprochement, however, although it possesses certain resemblances to the Christian tradition, also makes frequent, significant departures. The health and healing of individual persons are and always have been significant concerns in Christianity. Yet those concerns have always been understood to occupy a particular, limited place within the tradition's larger concern for its members to participate faithfully in the entire scope of God's redemptive work toward all of creation. Here we may turn to the writing of the church father Basil the Great, on whom we will also call later in this book. Basil at once acknowledges the legitimacy of the longing for health and at the same time warns against its disproportionate valuation: "And, when we were commended to return to the earth whence we had been taken and were united with the pain-ridden flesh doomed to destruction because of sin and, for the same reason, also subject to disease, the medical art was given to us to relieve the sick, in some degree at least." But: "Whatever requires an undue amount of thought or trouble or involves a large expenditure of effort and causes our whole life to revolve, as it were, around solicitude for the flesh must be avoided by Christians."[7]

This is a view quite different from the advocates of the contemporary rapprochement, who invariably claim that their work is scientific, not theological, and who say that the position they espouse is neutral with respect to any particular religious tradition. Apparently unaware of or unconcerned with the radical difference between the modern and Christian worldviews, they are likewise uninterested in the Christian tradition's measured valuation of health and its inherent opposition to the modern self-interested subject. Consequently, they often portray the desire for individual health as an end in itself. In so doing, they unwittingly give expression to a *particular* religion, one that represents a significant departure from Christian orthodoxy.

| | |

Religion and Medicine in Contemporary North American Culture

References to the religious disposition of contemporary Americans have become sufficiently common as to be uninteresting. Everyone has heard by now that Americans are the most religious people in the developed world and that they almost all believe not only in God but also in angels, heaven, miracles, and prayer. What pollsters and pundits less frequently articulate is the theological shape of contemporary American religiosity. In spite of frequent and sometimes strident claims to the contrary, most religious Americans are not Christians in any traditional sense. "There are indeed millions of Christians in the United States," says Harold

Bloom, "but most Americans who think that they are Christians truly are something else, intensely religious but devout in the American Religion, a faith that is old among us, and that comes in many guises and disguises, and that overdetermines much of our national life."[8] Americans, he goes on to explain, in spite of the fact that they often profess some sort of personal faith in Jesus, are not so much orthodox Christian as Gnostic. For as Bloom understands it, American religion

> has kept the figure of Jesus, a very solitary and personal American Jesus, who is also the resurrected Jesus rather than the crucified Jesus or the Jesus who ascended again to the Father. . . . The most Gnostic element in the American Religion is an astonishing reversal of ancient Gnosticism: we worship the Demiurge as God, more often than not under the name of manifest Necessity.[9]

Bloom's characterization of the American Religion as Gnostic is almost certainly exaggerated. Yet he is correct to insist that a great deal of American religiosity is a significant departure from historical Christianity. Contemporary Americans approach religion much in the same way they approach everything else: Americans are consumers, persons shaped from childhood to be particular kinds of what Rowan Williams calls "economic subjects."

> And what economic subjects do is commit their capital, limit their options by so doing, take risks for profit or gratification. They make property or assets take on meanings, values, in a pattern of exchange: things become a kind of language. Which is why, as a few metaphysicians have observed, economics is indeed an inescapable part of human business, one of the things we "just do" as human beings, as makers of meanings. Good: but the rhetoric of consumerism (the arts of advertising) necessarily softens the elements of commitment and risk. It is important to suggest that gain may be had with the minimum of loss. All advertising tends to treat its public as children—tends, that is, to suggest that decisions can be made without cost or risk.[10]

Religious practice in contemporary America is shaped by and large by consumerism, the latest stage of capitalism. Consumerism has shaped American religion in the sense that religion has for many become simply another aspect of life to be understood in terms of choice, acquisition, and exchange. It is a commodity among others, or at least a way of attaining commodities.[11] The point of the religious belief that is professed and practiced by most Americans is not that it is faithful to a particular historical tradition or even that it offers an intelligible account of the world in which they live. Americans want their religion first of all to be *helpful*—that is, they want it to be conducive to living a successful, worry-free life. One's religion need not be true except for the singular individual believer. Religion thus tends to be less about faithfulness to a tradition or a communal way of life than about individual empowerment.[12] "Urging the need for community on American religionists," Bloom observes, "is a vain enterprise; the experiential encounter with Jesus or God is too overwhelming for memories of community to abide, and the believer returns form the abyss of ecstasy with the self enhanced and otherness devalued."[13]

As one might expect in a culture where religiosity is at once ubiquitous, malleable, and radically individualized, the deity—or more frequently "faith" or simply "spirituality"—is often invoked as a means to achieve a variety of ends that are determined more by forces of the broader culture than by any one historic religious tradition. It should come as no surprise that, in a culture obsessed with youthfulness, self-empowerment, and in-dividual health, religion is increasingly advocated as a means of achieving or maintaining mental and physical wellness.[14] But such an account of religion, much less of health, has at best an ambiguous relationship to the Christian tradition.

| | |

Health and Culture

The suggestion that health and medicine are properly associated with one another is a truism. One need not look too closely at the history of medicine to see that where medicine has been practiced, its telos, that is, its goal, has been health. What is somewhat less obvious is the ways the particular beliefs, social practices, and ultimate expectations of specific cultures shape their understandings of what it means to be healthy and, consequently, of the medicine they practice. In this sense, health and medicine are part of the ideological framework of any given culture.[15] The way a particular culture understands what it means to be healthy and the place that culture gives to health among other goods tells us a great deal about what resources the members of that culture are willing to use to maintain or restore health. In contemporary North American culture, no less than any other, health and medicine tend to be viewed through particular ideological lenses. One of these is a scientific and technological optimism that sustains the tacit belief that science may one day altogether deliver us from sickness and death and every other limitation placed on us by our bodies.[16] Increasingly, we see a long, vigorous life as our inalienable birthright and medicine as the protector of that right. "Hardly anyone," says Daniel Callahan, "speaks openly of immortality as the aim [of medicine], but that is beside the point; it is built into the research imperative." Medicine's research imperative, he suggests, holds that:

> "Death is a series of preventable diseases." From this perspective, the researcher is like a sharpshooter who will pick off the enemy one by one: cancer, then heart disease, then diabetes, then AIDS, then Alzheimer's disease, and so on. The human-genome effort, the latest contender in the battle against death, will supposedly get to the genetic bottom of things, radically improving the aim of the sharpshooter.[17]

A second factor influencing our understanding of health and the expectations we place upon medicine is our radical individualism. Modern thought, political and scientific, is notoriously reductive. The fundamental unit of political thought is the self-interested, autonomous, rights-bearing individual, unencumbered by attachments to others except by choice.[18] Such a politics facilitates the tendency of those sciences on which modern medicine is built to school us to understand health on cellular, chemical, and individual rather than ecological levels. Consequently, most of us live with an understanding of health that is "fanatically individualistic."

> The body is seen as a defective or potentially defective machine, singular, solitary, and displaced, without love, solace or pleasure. Its health excludes unhealthy cigarettes but does not exclude unhealthy food, water, and air. One may presumably be healthy in a disintegrated family or community or in a destroyed or poisoned ecosystem.[19]

Both scientific and technological optimism and individualism are closely related to a third factor shaping our understandings of health and our expectations of medicine. We live in a consumerist political economy that at once shapes our desires and expectations and at the same time ostensibly offers us the means to fulfill them. In a general milieu of economic expansion and technological optimism, we are schooled to expect that the market and the laboratory, between them, will eventually solve all of our problems. "Capitalism itself, thanks to its growing dependence on consumerism, promotes an ethic of hedonism and health," and the "therapeutic sensibility," explains Christopher Lasch, "serves the needs of advanced capitalism as a whole."[20] The market promises us the things we want, including happiness and health and freedom from suffering and anguish, and just to the extent we participate in its enticements it continues to form us to expect even more of the same.

Our ever-expanding quest for physical and emotional health is especially influenced by these forces.[21] The same highly individualized health that is shaped by the expectation of endless technical and scientific progress is pursued as a consumer good among others, not simply through the commodity we know as medicine[22] but also through that contemporary peculiarity called "lifestyle," through interpersonal relationships, and through religious faith.[23] Lifestyle, relationship, and religion all come to be about the consumer and her desires. Indeed, observes John Kavanaugh, in late capitalist society these matters are all parts of the same whole.

> With consumerism functioning as a system of reality (a philosophy of what is most real and valuable) and a religion (a belief in what saves us and gives us ultimate meaning) it has occupied every piece of territory in our personal and social lives. Consumerism and its Commodity Form of life must be understood as an integrated unity that lives in and through, lives *off of*, our various experiences. One must comprehend it as a total world view, if one is to understand how it dwells in all the assorted parts of our lives. It does not just affect the way we shop. It affects the way we think and feel, the way we love and pray, the way we evaluate our enemies, the way we relate to our spouses and children. It is "systematic." It is "dialectical."[24]

None of this is to say that the human desire for physical and mental health is fundamentally misguided, or that medicine and religion should not both be fundamentally involved with their maintenance and restoration. Rather it is to suggest that the ways we finally understand what it means to be healthy and the ways we understand both medicine and religion to participate properly in our becoming or staying healthy are subject to profound distortion by the cultures of which we are members. But adjudications about the existence and extent of such distortions can only be made from the perspective of a particular way of life that offers a fulsome account of what it means to be healthy and what it means to be faithful and the way the two relate.

III

The Shape of the Christian Life
and the Place of Health in That Life

We experience the longing for health—that is, for wholeness—just to the extent that we are *not* healthy. Health is something we long for only when we do not have it, for health is finally nothing less than the entirety of our day-to-day flourishing as contingent beings in a contingent world. So long as we have longing, we are not absolutely healthy, for to experience longing is to be reminded that we are somehow incomplete. "Health," reminds Wendell Berry, "is at once wholeness and a kind of unconsciousness. Disease (dis-ease), on the contrary, makes us conscious not only of the state of our health but of the division of our bodies and our world into parts."[25] So health is concerned not just with the physical well-being of our individual bodies but also with the integrity of our being before God, our being with others, and our being in the world. We are not truly healthy so long as we are not at home with ourselves, at peace with our neighbors, and living harmoniously with that part of the earth we call home. As Berry puts it, "the community—in the fullest sense: a place and all its creatures—is the smallest unit of health and . . . to speak of the health of an isolated individual is a contradiction in terms."[26]

From this it would seem we are never healthy, for we experience almost continuously all sorts of unsatisfied longing. Some of the things we long for are inappropriate or simply bad for us, and we learn, if we are fortunate, how not to long for them. Others, if we are to believe those who have spoken for the Christian tradition, can and will be fulfilled only in the final completion of God's redemptive work beyond this life and this world. But it is absurd to expect that *all* of our longing is either sinful or else to be fulfilled only in the eschaton; to so deny the goodness of God's creation would be to engage in just another variation on the Gnosticism against which Christians have struggled from the beginning. We must therefore be able to say theologically that health is complex and extensive; there is a variety of interconnected ways for us to be healthy. Certain aspects of health of are attainable in this life, and then sometimes only fleetingly; others are attainable only in the next. Some are granted to us by our being good stewards of the creation, by being temperate and by living together in ways that avoid polluting the air, water, and soil on which we depend. Some come through medicine and other human enterprises, others through prayer and worship, and others through our caring presence to one another. All of these are God's good gifts. Thus it is wrong neither to long nor to strive for health, so long as both our longing and our striving are constrained by our being creatures who acknowledge that our lives are the good gifts of a gracious God who calls us to be his friends.

But of course, this is the very problem with which we began. If some of our longings are inappropriate and some are persistent reminders that our perfection is to be attained only in the eschaton and some are possibly to be satisfied here and now, then we must—if we wish to remain faithful—be able to discriminate among our desires and make judgments about the proper means to satisfy them. And in order to do this, we must begin with one of the fundamental tenets of the Christian tradition: All of our longings—right and wrong, ultimate and provisional—are somehow finally expressions of our longing to be made friends of the God who gives godself to the creation in the life and stories of Israel, Jesus, and the Church.

Until we are granted full and final participation in the life of the triune God, we will continue to experience desire. Until we begin the journey of discipleship toward full and final participation in that life, our experience of unfulfilled desire will be especially profound. "You have made us for yourself," prayed Augustine, who explained these matters as clearly as anyone, "and our heart is restless until it rests in you."[27] Until that time when we find rest in God, we will remain, as did Augustine, "vast problems" to ourselves,[28] for we desire a happiness that can finally be satisfied only by progress toward union with God.[29] This does not mean that our desires for things other than God are necessarily inappropriate; the desires we experience for things other than God—for pleasure, for human companionship, and for physical health, among others—are perfectly legitimate, insofar as they are expressions of and means to our desire for God.[30] The great challenge is to learn and practice the proper ordering of these desires:

> Some things are to be enjoyed, others to be used, and there are others which are to be enjoyed and used. Those things which are to be enjoyed make us blessed. Those things which are to be used help, and, as it were, sustain us as we move toward blessedness in order that we may gain and cling to those things which make us blessed. If we who enjoy and use things, being placed in the midst of things of both kinds, wish to enjoy those things which should be used, our course will be impeded and sometimes deflected, so that we are retarded in obtaining those things which are to be enjoyed, or even prevented altogether, shackled by an inferior love.[31]

Thus when we use the one thing that is of ultimate importance (God) purely or even primarily for the sake of getting less important—albeit still good—things, we are destined ultimately to experience radically unsatisfiable longing. For in so doing, we act out of desires that are fundamentally disordered: "To enjoy something is to cling to it with love for its own sake. To use something, however, is to employ it in obtaining that which you love, provided it is worthy of love. For an illicit use should rather be called a waste or an abuse."[32] Acting in such a way as to confuse the goods of creation with the Good that is friendship with God is a kind of idolatry; it is an injustice, not only to God but to ourselves and to the rest of the creation, as well.[33] Yet it would appear that such behavior if far from exceptional; it is much closer to being the rule, according to Nicholas Lash:

> All human beings have their hearts set somewhere, hold something sacred, worship at some shrine. We are spontaneously idolatrous—where, by "idolatry," I mean the worship of some creature, the setting of the heart on some particular thing (usually oneself). For most of us there is no single creature that is the object of our faith. Our hearts are torn, dispersed, distracted. We are (to use the seventeenth-century term) polytheists. And none of us are so self-transparent as to know quite where, in fact, our hearts are set.[34]

But in spite of the fact that we find ourselves in the grasp of such undue self-love, we are not without hope. Our desires can be reordered, and we can learn to love the right things at the right times in the right ways. This finally is one of the central meanings of Christian discipleship, "to know oneself apprenticed to a school the purpose of whose pedagogy is the purification of desire."[35] Being so purified does not mean, as we might be tempted to think, that we must renounce desire and cultivate sensibilities akin to Stoic *apatheia*. It means, rather, that our desire is released "from the chains which bind it in egotism's nervous and oppressive grasp."[36] Discipleship is a process of learning to love God and God's creatures well, understanding that "whatever we desire, our desiring of it is only the desire of God in the measure that it is conformed to and transformed by God's previous desire of us."[37] Only when we have learned to love well—to long for things in their proper order—will we have learned to live well.

III

A Well-lived Life—in Sickness and in Health

We began this introduction by asking what we properly ought to make of our persistent, eager longing for our lives to be other than they are—especially with regard to our experiences of sickness, pain, suffering, and death. We concluded by saying that so long as those desires were subordinated to our desire for God, they were simply part of what it means to be creatures living in a world alienated from its Creator, creatures free to imagine and pursue ways of fulfilling our longing. Yet we have not to this point said a great deal about what a life of properly ordered desires actually looks like. What, in concrete terms, does it *mean* properly to use the goods of creation to help achieve the Good of friendship with God—rather than the other way around—especially when we are sick and suffering?

For anything approaching a satisfying answer to this question, the reader must wait to read this book's final two chapters, where we try to articulate a theology of sickness and health that takes into account, but refuses to be determined by, the rise of modern medicine and the emergence of contemporary American culture. For now, we suggest that a life of properly ordered desires is a life that may be characterized as a friendship with the triune God; such a life is constituted by (at least) three characteristics.

First, a life lived in friendship with God is a life whose eager longing for the complete and final redemption of the body is circumscribed by the location of one's life within the rich narrative of God's saving acts in history. That narrative must be embodied communally in the church, through a kind of practical moral reasoning that is grounded in the life, death, and resurrection of Jesus of Nazareth. Indeed, if those strands of the Christian tradition we follow here are correct, then it is only within a community of human friends mutually committed to each other's flourishing that one can hope to become a friend of God.[38] Second, a life lived in friendship with God is one that acknowledges and embraces the properly interdependent nature of human existence. In this life, we are called as friends of God to be present in the community as servants to the suffering and weakness of others. Finally, a life lived in friendship with God is one that understands sickness and death as being in some sense part of, and not alien to, our lives as members of a fallen creation. Just so, we understand that although sickness and death are both enemies, neither are *ultimate* enemies.

In what follows, we will critically engage several contemporary popular accounts of the interrelationship between health and religious faith from the perspective of this characterization of the Christian life, asking whether and to what extent the methods and conclusions and especially the implicit theologies of these accounts enable or hinder faithful Christian discipleship. In so doing, we will be attempting to display what we understand to be a genealogy of contemporary associations between faith and health; we do this as a way of determining their validity, not as empirical truths but as theological ideas. In this sense, we share with Michael Buckley the conviction that:

> The genesis of a conviction is philosophically and theologically critical to its understanding if the idea is not reduced to a social product or a psychic inevitability, that is, if it is not explained or explained away by contraction to something else, if the ideational integrity of idea, argument, facts and principles is kept and submitted to a history and a critique on its own terms.[39]

We begin in chapter 1 by exploring the ambiguous history of the relationship between religious faith and medical practice, suggesting that the contemporary reemergence of a positive relationship has its basis less in theological conviction than in therapeutic utility. This is especially the case with those who advocate religious behavior *because* epidemiological studies have shown that religious people are generally healthier. We suggest at the end of chapter 1 that those who commend religion for its health benefits face some serious conceptual difficulties.

In chapter 2 we press this matter further by arguing that "religion" is a construct of modern thinking that in fact does not exist, at least not in the essential sense it is typically used. Consequently, the ongoing use of the notion of religion has significant theological repercussions. We posit in this chapter a genealogy of the development of the generic notion of "religion" that begins with a conceptual departure from the Christian narrative in the theology of sixteenth-century Europe and culminates with the work of the nineteenth-century philosopher Ludwig Feuerbach.

In chapter 3 we discuss the impact of Feuerbach's account of religion on the wider culture, including the very liberal Protestantism that he attempted to deconstruct. It is not incidental, we suggest, that Feuerbach was a significant influence on Karl Marx, who saw the very religion against which Feuerbach had launched his polemic as a force in the production of culture in modern capitalist political economies. Modern culture, we suggest, has come over time to be characterized by three traits: First, there is an abandonment of tradition, a subsequent moral fragmentation, and the emergence of a cult of the individual. Second, there is a fundamental trajectory toward narcissism, the tendency toward preoccupation with the self and its immediate status in the world. Finally, there is an emergence of a dominant therapeutic sensibility in which everything is evaluated in terms of its potential for facilitating the development of the individual self. Each of these traits is consistent with and facilitates the development of a general cultural attitude of consumerism, in which all things are understood as goods to be exchanged for the benefit of the exchanger.

In chapter 4 we turn to a constructive Christian alternative to this account of the relationship between religion and health. Here we say plainly what we have heretofore indicated only by allusion: that "religion" invariably tends to become idolatry, and health improperly pursued and valued is an idol, a false god. Here we rely on the work of two very different twentieth-century theologians. Karl Barth saw religion as being in some sense natural and at the same time a temptation to be resisted because of its tendency to be idolatry. John Milbank correctly understands capitalism as a religious tradition that can be properly critiqued not by Marxist theory but by Christian theology; Marx's vision of alienation overcome can only be realized in and through the life of the Christian community.

The resistance of idolatry that is the goal of Christian discipleship has its origins, we suggest, in an explicit turn to God's self-revelation in history. Following Barth, we suggest that the proper form of "religious" life is shaped in response to God's presence to the world in the life, death, and resurrection of Jesus of Nazareth. A life ordered in response to that presence understands finite human life in a fallen creation apocalyptically. To have an apocalyptic understanding of life, we explain, is to abandon the modern obsession with controlling the course of history and to live *hopefully*, with the certainty that the ultimate meaning of history—including each individual's personal history of sickness and of health—is determined not by scientific or religious cause and effect but by the cross and the resurrection of Christ.[40]

In chapter 5 we turn to scripture, literature, and poetry in an attempt to say something concrete about the shape of such a life. We begin by comparing the historical Christian tradition of ministry to the sick—including praying for their healing—to the thinking of the contemporary rapprochement, noting that the great difference between the two is that in the Christian tradition healing has been strictly understood not in terms of exchange but as pure gift. This is not to say that the Christian tradition has ever understood illness as *good* but that the Christian conflict with illness has taken the form not just of praying for healing but also, and especially, of showing patient hospitality to the sick and suffering.[41]

Whether those who are sick and suffering are healed by prayer or by medicine or whether they remain ill and experience the common fate of all creatures, one thing remains certain, "that we have no theological right to set any sort of limits to the loving-kindness of God which has appeared in Jesus Christ. Our theological duty is to see and understand it as being still greater than we had seen before."[42] And, we might add, to participate as fully as God enables in that lovingkindness.

Strange Bedfellows?

Reflections on a (Re)emergent Trend in American Healthcare

*Physic and faith criss-cross and overlap at many points; though often
complementary, there remains great potential for conflict; though separate,
there remains scope for unification.*

ROY PORTER

*Scripture and the theology of the church sustain the great maxim of the
theology of culture, that the soul of every culture is a religion and the body of
every religion is a culture; the gods are precisely "the gods of the nations."
They also maintain the prophetic critique that emerges from this
apprehension: just because the gods are each the god of a nation or race or
class or gender, they are "idols," products of our own religious subjectivity,
powers we envision by projection of our own values and needs.*

ROBERT JENSON

A mong the many things with which our culture is obsessed, the physical health of the individual and the capacity of science and scientific medicine to improve that health clearly rank near the top of the list.[1]
Collectively we worry almost continually about becoming ill, and we
hope, in the deepest recesses of our being, that mortality itself is an illness that will someday be cured.[2] Whether and in what ways these pre-
occupations are good or not remains to be seen, but we suspect that our

society's fantastic expenditures on healthcare and inordinate attention to the extension of life span and vigor are signs that we have lost our way and that we are, in ways more significant than we can imagine, a culture seriously diseased.[3] Nevertheless, we turn to medicine more than ever, with the hope that it can unravel and solve for us the deepest mysteries of what we believe are our all too mortal bodies.

And medicine itself has changed to meet our expectations, not only by becoming more adept at understanding, diagnosing, and treating those unhappy and undesirable conditions we have learned to call diseases, but by becoming increasingly responsive to the self-expressed needs of the "medical consumer." Whether in spite of or because of its technical sophistication and its sometimes immoderate scientism, medicine is now reconsidering the indifference to religion characterizing its recent past.[4] Physicians and others associated more peripherally with the healthcare enterprise—including sociologists, psychologists, health educators, and epidemiologists—have in the last twenty years or so begun systematically to reexamine the possibility that what they and their patients *believe*—about the existence and nature of God and about the nature of the world and the proper place of humans in the world—might make a significant difference where mental and physical health are concerned. Their studies appear at first glance to confirm what many people of faith have insisted all along: that religion does make a difference, one to which caregivers and patients alike might do well to attend.[5]

Yet it is difficult to say whether or to what extent medicine's emergent alliance with religion is really good news for people of faith. Given the highly individualized character of religious belief in contemporary American culture, the religion that medicine has (re)discovered may be no more than a simulacrum of any one of those several ancient, historical traditions we typically think of as religions.[6] While this point probably does not make much difference to those whose overarching concern is the physical well-being of the individual and the way religion can contribute positively to that health or to those concerned with meeting the needs of the medical consumer, it does matter theologically—at least to those of us who believe that theology has something to say about the way things really are.

Religious traditions make truth claims. Such claims are not only substantive but frequently totalizing. The claims many religious traditions make are not only or even primarily about the meaning and significance of human physical health but also about the proper conduct, nature, and destiny of all human and nonhuman life. And in most of the historical religious traditions, the latter takes precedence over and determinatively shapes the former. Religious traditions of this sort teach their adherents not so much how to be healthy and live long as how to live and die faithfully. Living and dying faithfully means living and dying in harmony with the deity, with other persons, and with the rest of the world—whether in sickness or in health. For the inordinate human propensity to get these reversed, prioritizing the immediate benefits of being religious over the requirements of faithfulness, many of those same traditions have a name: idolatry.[7]

This is not to say that from the perspective of those several traditions we commonly recognize as religions the contemporary association of faith with health is *necessarily* idolatrous. One way of understanding the contemporary rapprochement between religion and medicine is that it is simply the reestablishment of a very old concord. Our everyday words for health and holiness have common roots, as do those for healing and salvation. Many understand this shared etymology as a vestige of the time when people in many cultures understood their bodies and the forces that made them sick or well in terms and images that were at least implicitly religious.[8] For a long time in many cultures, both the individual human body and the social body of which the individual was a member were understood first of all as theatres of divine activity.

That understanding shaped the way those cultures cared for their sick. When a person became ill, she went for help not just to physicians but also to priests or shamans; often, in fact, these were the same people. As Roy Porter notes, in certain "highly unified or deliberately syncretist" cultures, there in fact never was a clear distinction *between* healers and religious leaders, and even in those somewhat later, more developed cultures that did make such distinctions, the "division of labour was never wholly sustainable."[9] For both the medical and religious leaders of the community were concerned not only with the "biological" phenomenon of the patient's illness but also with her place in the wider community and the integrity of her relationship to the deity, the other members of the community, and the rest of the creation. Each of the persons involved understood that this network of relationships had as much as anything to do with the patient's health. Treatment was consequently directed not just toward the diseased part of the patient's body but also toward reconciling the patient, "with self, with others, and with the gods or powers of nature. Such an emphasis on the whole person in community was and is characteristic of all religious healing traditions."[10]

But then—at least according to many of the standard accounts of the history of medicine—things changed.[11] Science discovered the real truth about the human body, and religious belief among patients came either to be dismissed as a superstitious obstruction to the enterprise of healing or disregarded as irrelevant to that enterprise—or simply ignored.[12] The new scientific medicine taught that the body was a kind of machine rather than a theatre of divine action; when a person became ill, it was because her machine was broken or contaminated by a material pathogen.[13] To be healed, the sick person went to a physician, who repaired the broken machine or removed or chemically destroyed the offending pathogen, increasingly without respect to anything other than the broken part or the offending pathogen. Even though there had always been people of faith among both patients and caregivers, medicine as an institution became increasingly uninterested in relating its mission to their belief. Religion and medicine, in spite of their long history of interdependence, came to operate in radically separate spheres, and physicians came increasingly to be seen as highly sophisticated technicians.[14]

These iatromechanical and iatrochemical models for understanding the body and its goods were radically successful, and their success was the primary force enabling their domination of medical thinking through the middle part of the twentieth century, when signs of change began to appear. According to the physician Larry Dossey, beginning around 1950, under rubrics such as holistic medicine or mind-body medicine, some within the healthcare professions began slowly to reconsider their disciplines' strict adherence to the canons of the sciences.[15] This is not to say that medicine suddenly became religious; medical thinking continued (and continues) to be dominated by the same positivist understanding of the body that emerged in the nineteenth century.[16] In spite of this, however, many believing patients and caregivers have always acted as if their belief made a difference where health is concerned. And all this belief, according to a rapidly expanding body of empirical research in epidemiology and the social sciences, has not been altogether unmerited. A series of comprehensive review articles published between 1987 and 1989 all agree in that they "present convincing evidence that rates of morbidity and mortality vary across religions and religious denominations, as well as less, but still somewhat consistent evidence that, on average, high levels of religious involvement are moderately associated with better health status."[17]

|||

The New Rapprochement between Medicine and Religion

The hundreds of empirical studies evaluating the effects of religious belief and practice on physical and mental health vary considerably in methodology, scientific rigor, and particular subject matter. Some studies attempt to correlate the health of their subjects with membership in some religious sect or another, others with participation in corporate and individual religious activities like worship or Bible studies, others with personal attitudes of spirituality or religiosity, and still others with the religiosity of persons other than the subjects.

The earliest studies suggesting a correspondence between religion and health were those focusing on "denominational differences in morbidity and mortality."[18] Various "behaviorally strict" communities, such as Mormons, Seventh-Day Adventists, and Hutterites, have typically been the focus of such studies.[19] Generally speaking, the members of these groups have been found to be significantly healthier than the general population, especially where illnesses determinatively related to intemperate lifestyles are concerned.[20] More recent studies based on religious group affiliation have employed less specific categories while continuing to focus on the way religious belief shapes ways of life. A 1990 study of cancer mortality rates attempting to determine "the effect of theology on health behaviors rather than in belief in particular religious values or norms" compared subjects based on their belonging to one of six groups: "conservative Protestant, moderate Protestant, liberal Protestant, Catholic, Jewish, and Mormon."[21] The findings of that study were significant: religious affiliation does make a difference where cancer mortality is concerned, and this difference "coincides generally with a religious continuum ranging from liberal to conservative."[22]

Increasingly, empirical studies of the relationship between religion and health have concentrated on the effects of religious belief per se by looking for a correspondence between personal religious activity—such as attendance at services, the study and devotional reading of sacred texts, or the practice of prayer and meditation—and various indicators of individual health. For example: One study, done by a well-established research group at Duke University, measures the response of the immune system in older adults to attendance at religious services, and finds "some support for the hypothesis that older adults who frequently attend religious services have healthier immune systems."[23] Another project conducted by the same researchers found a correlation between lower diastolic blood pressure and religious activities, including attendance at religious services, regular prayer, and personal Bible study.[24] Researchers have determined that older adults who regularly attend religious services spend less money on healthcare and less time in the hospital, a finding certain to earn the attention of cost-conscious healthcare systems.[25] Other studies show that religious people experience greater subjective well-being and that they have lower mortality rates when undergoing certain surgical procedures.[26]

| | |

Dissent within the Medical Community

This is not to say that medicine's newfound enthusiasm for religion is unequivocal. In a widely read and highly publicized 1999 article published in the *Lancet*, Richard Sloan and his colleagues comment on the "complex history" and the even more "complex present" of the relationship between religion and medicine. They offer a vigorous and even strident critique of certain elements of the new rapprochement, calling attention both to the quality of the empirical research associating religion with better health and especially to some of the ways researchers and their colleagues have used these studies.[27]

By suggesting the existence of methodological flaws in the conduct of many of these studies—especially their failure to account adequately for so-called confounding factors—Sloan and his colleagues call into question both the accuracy and the significance of the data obtained. Perhaps more significantly, they suggest that physicians who advocate significant clinical applications of the existing research to patient care may "abuse their status as professionals" by moving beyond the recognized limits of their expertise in their interactions with patients.[28] Although the *Lancet* article does not go so far as to say that religion should never be part of the patient–physician relationship, it does raise a morally and (for us) theologically significant point. There is, as the authors insist, a significant difference between a caregiver's "'taking into account' . . . religious factors and 'taking them on' as the objects of interventions." Given the limits of this culture's particular understanding of the physician–patient relationship, the physician's first obligation where religion is concerned is to respect that difference.[29]

Although Sloan and his colleagues offer the advocates of an increased involvement of religion with medicine two significant challenges, they are almost certainly too readily dismissive of the contemporary body of literature and the rich history of the interinvolvement of religion and medicine.[30] In spite of legitimate concerns over methodological rigor and interpretation, the empirical research does seem to show a consistent trend that cannot—and should not—be ignored. On the whole, studies show that "salutary effects of religious involvement persist despite an impressive array of statistical controls for social ties, health behaviors, and sociodemographic variables."[31] Religious people do seem to gain *some* health benefits from their belief. It is simply not clear, given the research that has been conducted, what is the extent of that benefit, how it should be explained, or what conclusions—if any—about its relevance to the practice of medicine should be drawn from it.

The authors of most of the individual epidemiological and empirical studies and comprehensive review articles are generally quite careful in their treatment of matters of interpretation and application. There is, says one review of these studies, clearly some sort of positive association between religion and health.[32] Given the sheer breadth of research, moreover, that association is almost certainly not a matter of chance.[33] At the same time, however, these authors warn against the conclusion that current research demonstrates that the divine persons or forces who are the objects of religious devotion are simply and efficiently the immediate cause of health among those who worship them.[34]

This is not to say these authors necessarily understand religion reductively. Several readily admit to being people of faith, and many clearly recognize that the social and behavioral aspects of religious traditions are no less "religion" than what might be called the nonempirical aspects.[35] They do, however, call attention to the existence of a broad range of possible explanations for the association of religion with better health. The existence of such a plurality of explanations suggests, they say, that physicians and others who would commend religion because it seems to have a salutary effect on health should proceed with caution.[36]

Some of the researchers involved with these studies go beyond advising caution; they warn stringently against the deductive misuse of existing research by those with any sort of interest in promoting religion. They point out that it is simply not accurate, for example, to say on the basis of current epidemiological research that religion promotes healing, that it keeps its practitioners from becoming sick, or that it is the most important sociological factor influencing physical well-being. And it is most certainly wrong to conclude that the current research proves the existence of a benevolent deity who heals or preserves health because of or in response to human devotion.[37] These are all theological claims that may or may not be true but are most certainly beyond the purview of epidemiological research or clinical practice.

But perhaps the most important lesson to be drawn from these warnings is the attention they call to the illogic of using widely variable epidemiological data to justify a new set of clinical interventions. It is one thing to note that the members of a particular community—people who share not just beliefs, but a set of practices constituting an entire way of life—live longer or spends less time in the hospital or less money on health care than the rest of us. It is another thing altogether to suggest—however implicitly—that particular persons who want to live longer or spend less time in the hospital or less money on on health care should for *those reasons* adopt the beliefs of that group. While the former is a legitimate, interesting, and perhaps meaningful observation about how an entire, complex way of life shared by a community of persons influences their health, the latter is likely to be a speciously utilitarian reduction of that way of life to a series of isolated techniques.

Yet this is precisely what an increasing number of those advocating a more religious medicine seem—sometimes in spite of their own disavowals of anything resembling such medically motivated proselytism—to suggest. In many cases, these authors are the same women and men who conduct the empirical studies. They begin with the observation that religion is important to most people, or that it has been shown to be conducive to better coping with illness, or that it is medically efficacious or a cost-effective way of helping patients get better. They then go on to argue for various kinds of incorporation of religion into different aspects of the healthcare enterprise, either by physicians or by patients or both. Because religious practices of various sorts are associated in various ways with better health, they reason, those practices ought to be understood by caregivers and patients alike as valuable healthcare resources among others.

And it is precisely here that the new rapprochement parts company with the traditional association of religion with medicine. In spite of the similarities, the new alliance is shaped less by the canons of faithfulness to the entirety of a particular religious tradition than by the consumerist forces of late modern culture. No longer are the ends, either of medical practice or religious faith, understood to be determined and articulated first of all by the concrete practices of specific historical religious communities. Rather, the final ends of both medicine and religion are increasingly determined by the desires of the individual consumer of medicine and religion, desires that are shaped in advance by the radically individualized consumer culture of this latest stage of modernity.[38] And when this is the case, both the practice of medicine and the historical religious traditions are affected for the worse by being rendered increasingly unintelligible.

By saying this we do not mean to suggest that the contemporary rapprochement is completely malignant theologically. Nor do we want to argue that those who advocate making religion an integral part of the healthcare enterprise are absolutely wrong. Rather, we think it is important to consider, by submitting them to theological scrutiny, the variety of ways that recent investigations of the effects of religious practice on health are being interpreted and promulgated. Our concerns are analogous to, but not identical with, those of Sloan and his colleagues. We concur that a clear distinction needs to be made between "taking into account" the possible influences of religion on health and "taking on" religion as a therapeutic intervention. It is problematic for physicians explicitly or implicitly to encourage patients to be more generically religious simply for the sake of improving health. Like Sloan, we are concerned with the violation of the distinction between "taking on" and "taking into account," as much for the ways such a violation might distort what it means to be religious as for the ways it might distort the physician—patient relationship. We think it is important to ask in individual cases who is advocating a more religious medicine, to whom, on what bases, and for what penultimate and ultimate reasons, all with an eye to the way particular answers to these questions might distort the notion of what it means to be faithful to a particular historical religious tradition.

In a very general way, those who advocate making religion a significant part of the healthcare enterprise may be divided into two groups, with a considerable tendency for the first to elide into the second. The first group is made up of those who believe that religion is significant, insofar as religious commitments are among the several things that make certain patients the persons they are. Because physicians should know their patients in order to care for them properly, physicians should know about their patients' religious commitments. Because religion is an irreducible part of what it means for those patients to be healthy human beings, physicians who in various ways facilitate their patients' religiosity are making an indirect contribution to their overall health.

The second group includes those who write to lay as well as professional audiences and who reason that since the research shows that religion seems to effect better health, then being more religious is a good thing, if for no other reason than to promote better health. Generally speaking, we find in the current literature relating religion and health a strong tendency—albeit certainly not an absolute one—toward a theologically problematic, utilitarian account of religion. This is especially the case with those more popular and anecdotal works that most plainly commend religiosity or spirituality *for* its health benefits and so offer an account of religious faith that is, at least from the perspective of the Christian tradition on behalf of which we write, idolatrous.

| | |
Wholism: Asking the Right Questions
to Treat the Complete Patient

An expanding body of literature claims that physicians and other care-givers, if they wish to offer their patients complete and authentic care, must know their patients as *persons* and not just as diseased bodies or collections of diseased body parts.[39] This commendation suggests that physicians should know at least something about patients' religious commitments. Given the broad tendency in contemporary medicine to think of the body strictly in terms of the physical and natural sciences, this may seem a strange notion. Medicine, after all, is properly concerned with the body, while religion is concerned with the soul; medicine with what can be demonstrated, religion with what might be believed. But even on philosophical grounds, these distinctions are highly suspect.[40] Therefore, there may well be good reasons for physicians to know about their patients' religious commitments, regardless of whether the current literature says there is a positive relationship between faith and health.

To be human is to be a body. In itself this is not reductionism, for the body, properly understood, is more than a machine that is reducible to its constituent parts.[41] To be a human body is to live as an embodied agent who is interdependent with particular, embodied others and with a world that is in its own right and in many ways alive. Thus health and illness are never only about the presence or absence of disease. "Health is not just the sense of completeness in ourselves but also is the sense of belonging to others and to our place; it is an unconscious awareness of community, of having in common."[42] Medicine, if it is to be successful, must take this into account; it must move beyond the limits imposed by understanding the body as a machine. So long as medicine fails to do this, it "manifestly cannot grasp the full reality of its object, man, or learn how to use its knowledge morally or humanely without relaxing its positivist bias."[43] Medicine is not the interaction between a person and a thing but between a person and a person; it is, in the words of Edmund Pellegrino and David Thomasma, "an interhuman event."[44]

Because the patient is never simply an object, the physician should always take into account that the patient is not fully reducible to the categories and data provided by scientific investigation of the body.[45] Certainly there is a continuity of the person with these categories and data. But there is also a fundamental distinction between what Pellegrino and Thomasma call the *living body*—that aspect of the physical self that can legitimately be treated as an object and understood scientifically—and the *lived body*, the aspect through which the person as a historically particular agent presents herself to the world.[46] In order for a physician to make a sound clinical judgment on behalf of a particular patient, she must account to the extent she can for the particularity of that patient's lived body. A physician must, that is, know not only the objective scientific data about her patient but also the specific way the patient's history as a particular social agent who lives and moves and has her being in and through a particular web of relationships with other social agents makes her the person she is.[47]

The attainment of such knowledge comes, among other ways, through that clinical conversation between physician and patient in which the physician attends to "a whole series of questions . . . crucial for [the patient] as a knowing and valuing human being."[48] Schematically, say Pellegrino and Thomasma, these are reducible to three "generic" questions. These are: a diagnostic question ("What can be wrong?"); a general therapeutic question ("What can be done?"); and a final, critical question of clinical judgment, in which the physician accounts for the patient *as* a particular lived body by asking, "What *should* be done for *this* patient?"[49]

If we employ this model for making clinical judgments, it is not unreasonable to suggest that in moving from the diagnostic question to the critical question, the discerning physician ought to give consideration to the religious commitments of her patients, quite apart from what the physician believes—or what empirical studies show—about the possible therapeutic benefits of those commitments. Such commitments, which typically encompass *at least* a common canonical narrative and a particular set of social relations and habitual practices shared by the patient with his or her coreligionists, are by any account a significant part of what makes a given person the lived body he or she is.[50] Apart from her belief, a patient would in some sense be someone else. Her lived body and therefore her treatment, given Pellegrino and Thomasma's model, might well need to be different.

So those who advocate making the patient's religious commitment a legitimate and even a vital part of the clinical conversation between physician and patient have a point. Many patients believe, and by several accounts they want those who care for them to know that they believe and what they believe and to take their beliefs into account in deciding what care to offer them—even in those cases where the caregivers themselves do not believe.[51] But it is one thing to say that caregivers should take their patients' beliefs into account and another to specify how that taking-into-account should proceed and whether and what kind of limits should be placed on it.

A physician can make herself aware of the existent religious commitments of her critically, chronically, or terminally ill patients. As she does so, she can make some accommodations clinically to facilitate the exercise of those commitments, for instance, by providing or even encouraging appropriate access to her patients' clergy.[52] Such interventions would seem to be based simply on sound clinical judgment, regardless of whether the physician thought religion was medically a good thing or not. Given that these may not typically be matters of conversation between physicians and patients, however, it is not clear how the physician should best go about learning of her patients' religious commitments or how clinically important it is for every physician to know about the commitment of every patient. On these points, advocates of a more religious medicine differ, and some begin the slide down a slippery slope from being advocates of accounting fully for the particularity of each patient to advocating religion because the physician believes it has been shown to be medically beneficial.

In a review article published in the *Archives of Family Medicine*, several of the more enthusiastic advocates of a more religious medicine offer physicians a set of guidelines for addressing religious matters. These guidelines are ostensibly based on the authors' understanding that "the published research suggests that religious commitment might play a role in enhancing illness prevention, coping with illness and recovery." Physicians, they say, "might adopt several practices that will help them assess the health-relevant aspects of patients' religious commitment."

First, family physicians might integrate 2 questions into their initial interview. Clinicians might ask, "Is your religion (or faith) helpful to you in handling your illness?" If the answer is yes, they might follow with the question, "What can I do to support your faith or religious commitment?" Were physicians to ask these questions (and appropriate follow-up questions) more routinely in medical care, they would gain access to potentially valuable information on how to integrate religious factors into the care plans of particular patients—particularly those patients suffering from chronic or severe mental illness.[53]

The language used here shows nicely the difficulty a physician in a fragmented world such as our own faces in making and respecting the distinction between taking religion into account and taking it on because of its possible therapeutic benefits. It also alludes to the more theologically significant problem of how such necessarily generic assumptions about religiosity and its effects on health tend always to distort the character of any particular religious tradition. When a physician asks her patient whether the patient has religious commitments and whether those commitments are significant ways for the patient to deal with illness, she is asking a potentially important, open-ended question. The physician learns about who the patient is as a lived body, and the patient remains free to respond or not respond. Because the patient retains some control over the nature and extent of the response, her religious commitments remain her own, formed by her sharing in the narratives and participating in the practices of her particular religious tradition.

But when a physician becomes an *advocate* of a particular patient's religious commitments, whether by asking how she can support the patient's religious commitment or by more overtly encouraging those commitments, she is doing something besides simply learning about who the patient is in order to make better decisions about treatment.

> Where appropriate, religious patients might be encouraged to pray more—whether individually or with others. If already attending a church, synagogue, or mosque, they might be encouraged to continue. They might be encouraged to meditate. They might be encouraged to attend worship, engage is religiously based mourning rituals, seek and ask forgiveness from significant others, or read holy writ. In short, it would seem that many religious practices that patients find potentially meaningful and congruent with their own value systems might become resources for enhanced prevention, coping, and recovery.[54]

In this case, a shift—albeit a subtle one—has taken place. Religion now occupies a different space in the physician–patient relationship, because the physician has moved from simply learning about her patient's religious commitments to being an advocate of her patient's being religious. This is not necessarily wrong; medicine, because it is an interaction between two persons, always has about it an element of the dramatic. Just so, as important as it is for a physician to respect the autonomy of her patient, the physician's role will always in part be rhetorical. "Argument based on knowledge does not always produce desired results, because some people cannot be fully instructed on the topic. In these cases persuasion is necessary."[55]

But this does not mean that the physician's every rhetorical effort is justifiable, even if she is persuaded that there is legitimate scientific evidence showing that more religious patients have better medical outcomes. The physician needs to remain mindful of the possibility that she is being coercive or doing violence to the patient and whatever existent commitments the patient may possess prior to the clinical encounter:

Scientific and semiscientific conclusions of varying degrees of certitude are examined under a light strongly tinged with moral hues. The accessibility of the questions to scientific modes of reasoning declines, as does the degree of certitude, as we move from determining what *is* wrong, to what *can* be done, to what *should* be done. The optimization of several kinds of uncertainty remains a central concern even when the conclusions are scientifically defensible.[56]

Whether it is appropriate or not for a physician to advocate being religious to a patient (for whatever reason) is thus a matter of practical judgment about whether this or that set of religious commitments will enable the patient to flourish.[57] But such judgments about what enables flourishing depend largely on the patient and physician having a common sense of what it means to flourish. And because the body and its good is not reducible to data—that is, because there is no complete account of health that is not particular to some historically contingent way of narrating the body and its good—such common sense is typically acquired by participation in a common tradition. Traditions teach their members what it means to flourish; many of them also correct those members' most common misperceptions about whether particular accomplishments or pursuits are in fact constitutive of flourishing. By teaching members which of their many desires should be pursued and which should be abandoned, such traditions teach members to distinguish between faithfulness and idolatry and between truthfulness and self-deception. And by giving them ways to understand themselves as flourishing apart from or in spite of unhappy contingencies like sickness—contingencies that at first glance make flourishing improbable or impossible—those traditions offer their members real alternatives to the blind pursuit of freedom from contingency.

So if the physician and patient discover in the course of the clinical conversation that they are members of a common religious tradition, we would expect them to talk about how the patient's illness may be understood and addressed in light of how that tradition shapes its members to think about health, illness, suffering, and death.[58] That is, we would expect them to deliberate and perhaps even to argue about how their shared tradition provides ways for its members to flourish—that is, to live well—even in he midst of sickness. And even if they do not share religious commitments, a physician's encouragement of her patient's already existent beliefs might be nothing more than the physician's "giving permission" for a patient freely to be the person she is.

But things are altogether different if the physician and the patient do not share a common understanding of what it means to flourish. If either or both of their understandings of human flourishing and the role health has in enabling a good life derive from the dominant contemporary sensibility, which thinks of health solely as the absence of disease and flourishing as the related capacity of the individual to pursue his or her privately chosen way of life, then it is likely that the notion of religion they associate with better health will also have contemporary origins. It will be something other than one of those historical religious traditions that have as their goal to be "schools whose pedagogy has the twofold purpose—however differently conceived and executed in the different traditions—of weaning us from our idolatry and purifying our desire."[59]

|||

Religion as Cure: Medicine Seizes Faith

While there is in the contemporary popular literature advocating religiosity because of its association with better health no formally agreed-on definition of what "religion" is, there is a constellation of assumptions that make for a commonly held working understanding. First, religion is understood and articulated primarily as a function of individual human subjectivity. Religiosity is, in other words, an a priori capacity possessed by every human individual. Consequently the emphasis in most of this literature is on the act of believing—however "believing" happens to be understood by a particular author—rather than the particular object of belief. The old saw "Everybody needs to believe in something" fits especially well here. The second assumption flows from and is dependent on the first. Religion *as such* operates as a comprehensive, exhaustive, and ostensibly theological neutral category. This means that categories "religion" and "belief" are more determinative, for example, than categories such as "Islam," "Judaism," "Christianity," or "Buddhism." Third, religion is viewed instrumentally and reductively, meaning it is understood to be not so much a good way of life in itself as a means, among others, of helping an individual achieve whatever he or she believes is a good life for him or her.[60]   *disagree*

Even among those whose work has been concerned mostly with "traditional religious faith and practice," the decided emphasis in most of the popular literature on religion and health is on the act of believing and the effects of that act, rather than the particular object of belief.[61] Believing is understood primarily as an act of the human will. As such, the object of belief is less the one who creates or enables the act of believing than the product of that act. In his book *The Healing Power of Faith*, Harold Koenig remarks that for the religious patients with whom he has worked, faith is:

> The confident belief in a supreme being, which most call God. For them, God is loving and accessible. This is a God who listens to prayer, who responds, who desires good for humanity. This is an *intentional* God who sets goals we can strive toward to reach our highest potential in terms of physical, mental and spiritual health—which aren't always achieved in that order. Those with faith in this God rarely feel lost or abandoned or experience the psychological anguish we call "anomie," a condition that afflicts millions in our fast-paced, affluent world.[62]

Such faith offers believers "a tangible sense of mastery in their lives." It is a "reserve of energy and motivation that allows them to persevere."[63] Belief, in this account, is a powerful capacity that, when actualized, according to the Harvard physician Herbert Benson, "can create . . . internal environments that can help the individual reach enhanced states of health and well-being."[64] Belief so understood is primarily a human potential, as Benson suggests:

> most of us have little idea how great our "performance ceiling" is, both physically and mentally. *If you truly believe in your personal philosophy or religious faith—if you are committed, mind and soul, to your world view—you may well be capable of achieving remarkable feats of mind and body that many only speculate about.*[65]

Such faith as can affect human achievement can have any number of objects, so long as those objects are positive and conducive to the achievement of better health. Benson is especially clear on this point. Drawing on studies of the so-called placebo and nocebo effects, he indicates that where faith and health are concerned, the central issue is the act of believing. Negative beliefs tend to produce negative outcomes, whereas positive beliefs, regardless of the precise material content of their particular object, tend to produce positive outcomes.

> Apparently, just *having* a strong belief is enough to cause things to happen in our physiology, but this is a very ticklish point. It does seem that just the state of belief, which can emanate from a variety of personal, philosophical, or religious orientations, is itself a powerful force. Does it matter what you believe in? Belief in *something* is crucial. The very force and effectiveness of your personal belief stem

But in what?

from your basic assumptions that your belief matters. If you want to experience the physiological benefits of the Faith Factor and you find you have nothing to believe in, it may be helpful to believe generally in the power of life or perhaps even just in the power of belief itself.[66]

A religious faith that is understood primarily as a function of universal human subjectivity is necessarily theologically neutral with respect to any particular religious tradition. Because the contemporary rapprochement has its origins at least partly in recent social scientific and epidemiological research, it is directed by the canons of that research toward a broader, more generic understanding of religion and of faith than any one tradition would ordinarily permit.[67] Since the act of believing is transcultural and transhistorical, the capacity of faith to influence health exceeds any limitations placed on it by any particular historical religious tradition.[68] The objects of all particular beliefs are reducible to a universal core, as in this passage from Benson's work: *example?*

> I describe "God" with a capital "G" in this book but nevertheless hope readers will understand I am referring to all the deities of the Judeo-Christian, Buddhist, Muslim, and Hindu traditions, to gods and goddesses, as well as to all the spirits worshipped and beloved by humans all over the world and throughout history. In my scientific observations, I have observed that no matter what name you give the Infinite Absolute you worship, no matter what theology you ascribe to, the results of believing in God are the same.[69] *disagree*

positive thinking?

This is a point of particular emphasis for those who are convinced that faith improves health. Because the faith they speak of has its origins in individual human subjectivity, it is fundamentally private and personal. Consequently it is largely beyond the reach of critical theological judgments with regard to its content. Such faith is supposedly genuinely universal and embraces all particular faiths. In this sense it is decidedly mystical. "As all the major esoteric wisdom traditions tell us," says Larry Dossey, "the absolute 'cannot be spoken or thought.' There are simply no reliable pictures of the Almighty."[70] Consequently, he suggests, particular names for and images of "the Absolute" are merely preferences.[71] God may be called whatever one pleases to call God, for, in the words of the German mystic Meister Eckhart, "It is God's nature to be without a nature."[72]

As opposed to the universal faith of the contemporary rapprochement, which is concerned to account for the most recent scientific advancements, traditional models of faith, religion, and religious activities such as prayer are scientifically and politically—and hence theologically—outdated. Clearly theology here is understood to be in the service of science and politics and not the other way around. Traditional models of belief are fundamentally intolerant; just as important, they fail to account for the scientific evidence, which shows "that prayer does not belong exclusively to any particular religion, but to a unity of all religions, classes, and creeds."[73] A nontraditional paradigm is called for, one that uses the latest scientific research to advance a newer, more useful theology.[74]

The old biblically based views of prayer, which are still largely in vogue, were developed when a view of the world was in place that is now antiquated and incomplete. In this century our fundamental ideas about how the universe works have changed. We have redefined our ideas about space, time, energy, and causation. These bear little resemblance to the views that dominated human thought for millenia in the West, and that shaped our concepts of prayer. In addition, our basic ideas of the structure and function of the human psyche have been radically transformed and continue to evolve. If our world view has changed, perhaps we should also reevaluate our views of the nature of prayer.[75]

The desire for a universal, personal religion untainted by the particularity of theological tradition is clearly related to the attempt to offer an account of a religion that is useful, in these cases for the improvement of health. Thus for many advocates of the contemporary rapprochement, the only permissible criteria for judging the theological content of any particular set of religious commitments have to do with those commitments' medical utility.[76] An important part of Benson's work concerns the so-called nocebo effect, which is simply the inverse of the well-known placebo effect. Simply put, placebo/nocebo means that beliefs, whether positive or negative, produce nonspecific physiological effects.[77] Positive beliefs tend to produce positive physiological outcomes, while negative beliefs produce negative outcomes. Beliefs can preserve life or they can cause death, depending on their content.[78]

Because belief has been shown to have the capacity to effect both positive and negative medical outcomes, the content of belief matters from a strictly medical perspective.[79] This leads to a strong utilitarian account of belief, the logic of which is fairly obvious. If what a person believes promotes health, those beliefs should be encouraged; if what they believe is deleterious to health, those beliefs should be discouraged or modified.

So the act and the utility of believing something positive tends to be

than what is believed

valued above any consideration of the ultimate truthfulness of what is believed. Indeed, utility and truthfulness are in most cases no longer distinguishable. The primal act of belief, because it is thought to be a scientifically demonstrable part of human being, is more significant and more inherently "truthful" than the content of any particular belief. Moreover, "the divine is a luxury that cannot be afforded except as it submits to human demands, is totally identified with human knowledge and intention, as aesthetic possibility, or is a domesticated servant of success and self-esteem."[80] What matters are the tangible effects of faith; as Benson remarks, "we may reject the logic of God but we cannot deny the emotional and physical solace of spiritual life."[81]

Belief, or the exercise of the "spiritual life," produces an effect Benson calls "remembered wellness." Remembered wellness is a fundamental human instinct for health, the "most influential form" of which is belief in God. This is not necessarily an explicitly theological point: "Whether we 'remember' the peace of God because God wants us to, or we 'remember' a life-transcending power because our evolution made it requisite a requisite for survival, faith in a supreme being is a supreme physical healer."[82] And this assertion is not simply indicative but also hortative. Making dubious use of Anselm's famous ontological argument for the existence of God, Benson advises those with an interest in harnessing the healing power of belief: "So whether or not you believe in God per se, try to conceive of greatness beyond which there can be nothing greater."[83]

So even though individuals believe *in* a variety of different things, they all have in common the fact of their belief; everyone believes in *something*. In fact, that believing may not need to be especially substantive. Koenig remarks: "Even if you lack strong faith, you might gain considerable health benefits by observing devoutly religious people and adopting some of their practices, perhaps community volunteer work."[84] The research showing that belief can benefit health has practical application "even for those who lack religious belief entirely."[85]

belief in what.

III

The Problem with Being Generically Religious

We have broadly characterized the "religion" proffered by the advocates of the contemporary rapprochement of religion and medicine, saying that it is generally and for the most part subjectivist, theologically non-particular and purportedly neutral with regard to objective doctrinal content, and instrumental in the sense that it is oriented toward the achievement of goods external to the religion itself. Such an understanding of religion approximates what the theologian George Lindbeck has called "experiential-expressive." Experiential-expressive interpretations of religion focus on the experience of the religious person, interpreting "doctrines as noninformative or nondiscursive symbols of inner feelings, attitudes, or existential orientations."[86] The relationship btween doctrine and the subjective act of believing takes place, in the experiential-expressive understanding, "from the inside out." Given that relationship, the content of belief is ambiguous and always subject to change.

> The general principle is that insofar as doctrines function as nondiscursive symbols, they are polyvalent in import and therefore subject to changes of meaning or even to a total loss of meaningfulness, to what Tillich calls their death. They are not crucial for religious agreement or disagreement, because they are constituted by harmony or conflict in underlying feelings, attitudes, existential orientations, or practices, rather than by what happens on the level of symbolic (including doctrinal) objectifications.[87]

This understanding of religion is deeply rooted in modern culture, where, according to Lindbeck, "the structures of modernity press individuals to meet God first in the depth of their souls."[88] Modernity's egalitarian impulse and its broad suspicion of traditional authority, its recognition of an ascendant scientific reason as the only legitimate arbiter of public (i.e., "real") truth, and its subsequent acceptance of the deep division between the public and private realms all combine to give rise to a general sense that religious belief is a private matter and that it cannot and should not be judged with respect to its content.

Because belief is with respect to its objective content understood to be nondiscursive, differences in content are held by those whose faith might be characterized as experiential-expressive to be nothing more than "different expressions of a common core experience."[89] And since "the experience [of belief] is the source and norm of objectification," then the object of experience may be judged only with reference to the experience, which is presumed always and everywhere to be more significant than the experience itself.[90]

And because, at least in a highly individualized, liberal democratic regime such as our own, experience is understood as *originating with* and *belonging to* the individual, the experience itself is largely beyond the reach of judgment. To put it perhaps a bit too crudely, a good religion is one that corresponds to a good experience, where what makes for a "good experience" is to be defined first of all—and perhaps even *only*—by the experiencing subject, according to her desires. Thus increasing numbers of people regard all religions as possible sources of symbols to be used eclectically in articulating, clarifying, and organizing experiences of the inner self. Religions are seen as multiple suppliers of a single commodity needed for transcendent self-expression and self-realization.[91]

Lindbeck observes that the experiential-expressivist model, despite its prevalence in the modern West, cannot fully account for what it has traditionally meant to "be religious." In the main, he says, being religious has been understood as something requiring a kind of systematic training, analogous to learning a language and the way that language functions within a corresponding form of life. In this way, religions are more like cultures than feelings, and doctrines are not so much nondiscursive expressions of private inner experiences as they are "communally authoritative rules of discourse, attitude, and action" that teach one to live well as a citizen of a particular religious culture.[92]

This "cultural-linguistic" account of religion, in which "religions are seen as comprehensive interpretive schemes, usually embodied in myths or narratives and heavily ritualized," does not disregard or deny the existence of human religious experience. Rather, it denies the primacy and the priority of *individual* religious experience by showing that the myths, narratives, and rituals that make up a particular way of life themselves "structure human experience and understanding of self and world."[93] It is not the naked experience of an individual's believing in something beyond the self that gives rise to the description of that experience and the accompanying religious way of life; it is the way of life of this or that religious community or culture that gives rise to the description and makes possible an individual experience that can be described as religious.[94] "A religion is in the cultural-linguistic understanding above all an external word, a *verbum externum*, that molds and shapes the self and its world, rather than an expression of a preexisting self or a preconceptual experience."[95]

Now this is not simply an esoteric debate among philosophers of religion about whether being religious is better described as a phenomenon occurring from the "inside out" or the "outside in". According to the experiential-expressivist account of religion, the essential core of religiosity, the individual religious experience, is merely *contained within* some or another historically contingent, external form that is finally superfluous to the experience itself. The shape of the contingent form can (and does) change, and this without altering the essential core experience of belief or diminishing its utility. And because all particular religious commitments are expressions of a singular core experience, then all particular religious commitments are, when properly understood, finally the same, which is to say, they are insignificant.

But if language and the descriptions enabled by language are basic elements *of* human experience—that is, if they enable and shape human experience—then the cultural-linguistic account of religion is more descriptively accurate than the experiential-expressivist.[96] Those allegedly nondiscursive aspects of religion that experiential-expressivists see as mere preferences or as accidents of history are in fact fundamental to what it means to "be religious" in a particular way. If they are changed, then the religion itself is changed—and may, in fact, become a different religion. So the modern account of religion proffered by the advocates of the new rapprochement turns out not to be theologically neutral at all, for religion is never religion as such but always a *particular* religion. The freely chosen, utilitarian religion of individual experience is the particular religion of capitalist high modernity.

Just so, writers like Benson, Dossey, and Koenig, for all their remarkable insights and good intentions, are simply wrong when they claim that, in their suggestions about how to use faith to improve health, that they are—to use Koenig's words—"*not* offering spiritual counseling here, but rather trying to provide advice to enhance the health benefits of faith, based on this scientific research."[97] They *are* offering spiritual advice. Because faith does not exist apart from its being a way of living with respect to some discursive object, those who advocate faith for its health benefits are explicitly advocating faith in the discursive object that is defined in part by its giving health in exchange for religiosity. That is, they are advocating a *particular religion*—albeit one that is vaguely defined and nontraditional—with its own particular account of the ends of human life and its own implicit doctrine of God, humanity, and the rest of the creation. The particular religion they advocate may or may not in the final analysis lead to better health, but it is not, finally, identical with Christianity or Judaism or any other religion, except itself, the religion that offers better health to those faithful to its canons.

|||

Health and the Religion of American High Modernity

Despite its being vaguely construed, the religion of the contemporary rapprochement does have an identifiable (minimal) material content in addition to the formal characteristics just described.[98] This religion is clearly a product of several of the forces of late modernity and bears a strong resemblance to what Harold Bloom has named the "American Religion," a contemporary variation on the ancient Christian heresy called Gnosticism. In particular, the religion of the contemporary rapprochement is, like Bloom's American Religion and the Gnosticism from which it descends, radically individualistic. "Urging the need for community on American religionists," Bloom remarks, "is a vain enterprise; the experiential encounter with Jesus or God is too overwhelming for memories of community to abide, and the believer returns from the abyss of ecstasy with the self enhanced and otherness devalued."[99]

Gnostic or not, such a radically individualized religion leads in a fairly straightforward way to a religion that is relatively uncritical with respect to individual desires. To employ a pair of overused idioms from popular psychology, the religionist's "felt needs" are generally and for the most part equated with their "real needs." Desires, like beliefs, are understood to have their origins within the individual, and the individual is generally regarded as having the sovereign right to author the story of her own life. As such, religion is less a way of systematically *reshaping* desire, of differentiating felt need from real need, than it is a means of *fulfilling* desire.[100] Religion in modernity is characterized by what Hans Frei called the "great reversal," in which religion went from creating a narrative world into which the religious person was obligated to make her life fit to being an apologetic for her life as it was.[101] Religion thus gradually becomes a means of achieving whatever desires the religionist happens to possess. "In the self-assured world of modernity, people seek to make sense of the Scriptures, instead of hoping, with the aid of the Scriptures, to make some sense of themselves."[102]

Such religion as is concerned with addressing the felt needs of the religionist is uncritical with respect to those needs because—and just to the extent that—it remains naive about their source. Michel Foucault and Alasdair MacIntyre have taught us about the subtle ways the various forces of modern culture and especially of capitalist political economy shape our subjectivity by training us to value or desire some things to the exclusion of others, masking themselves all the while as merely our autonomous choices.[103] And it is certainly the case that in the most recent stage of American modernity, the exponentially growing influence of consumerism—the sense that every aspect of life is finally best understood according to the logic of self-interested economic exchange—is a fundamental aspect of this shaping.

America is the nation invented by Enlightenment philosophers; just so it is the paradigmatic capitalist nation. Capitalist theories, which elsewhere have functioned as hypotheses to be followed when they work, have in America the status of founding and inviolable myth. Thus what elsewhere is only description of certain ways of participating in the market comes in America to carry moral and even *religious* weight: entrepreneurship or accumulation of wealth are seen as goods in themselves.[104]

Thus the idealized story of the liberal state and its capitalist political economy becomes *the* religious story in America.[105] It is not simply that capitalist political economies make virtue of vice by teaching those who live in them universally to embrace the acquisition of wealth as the human telos, although there are certainly considerable pressures in that direction. It is that capitalism forms and informs the logic of *every* judgment of those who uncritically participate in it, and especially of their interactions with one another. Anything desirable is or ought to be attainable through exchange. There is a subtle pressure for everything to be viewed as a commodity and a pressure for all questions, religious questions included, to be reduced to questions of utility. And so religious apologists for capitalism make theologically absurd claims, such as Michael Novak's pseudo-Christian assertion that: "The point of Incarnation is to respect the world as it is . . . and to disbelieve any promises that the world is now or ever will be transformed into the City of God."[106]

It is finally impossible for a religion so directed toward the satisfaction of immediate desire and so naive about the sources of that desire to be prophetic. If individual health is for whatever reason valued uncritically as a good of the dominant culture, then it is automatically valued as a good of the religion, as well. Such a religion cannot serve, as Nicholas Lash has suggested religion properly should serve, as a school "whose pedagogy has the twofold purpose—however differently conceived and executed in the different [religious] traditions—of weaning us from our idolatry and purifying our desire."[107] In fact, it becomes questionable whether from the perspective of such a religion it even makes sense to speak any longer of idolatry. Religion cannot tell me whether I ought to want the things I want, or in what order I should want them, or whether there are things I should not do to attain them; it can only serve as a means to help me get them.

Religion so conceived is almost purely therapeutic, not in the sense that its purpose is the cure of the soul or the enabling of genuine flourishing—in which cases "'blessedness' is always to be defined by the moral will of the Lord"[108]—but in the sense of what it can provide with respect to the preexisting desires of the religionist. The therapeutic ethos is pervasive in American religion, and especially in its ostensibly Christian manifestations. "In taking the therapeutic option," remarks Gary Dorrien, "modern Christianity builds upon a considerable American tradition of building the world out of the self."[109] He observes:

> Most Americans may believe in God, but this affirmation does not lead most of them to make serious commitments to any community of faith or distinctively Christian ethic. Modern American religion abounds with prescriptions to help anxious consumers get in touch with their feelings, relinquish negative thoughts, and rediscover the child within themselves.[110]

To Dorrien's characterization, we might add that modern American religion now abounds with prescriptions to help anxious consumers free themselves and remain free of the effects of disease and aging. The original concord between religion and medicine has been turned upside down. Whereas religion once taught its adherents to worship God, whether in sickness or in health, and to use medicine to live with the world and with one another in a way that encouraged that worship, religion now teaches its adherents to worship their desire for health and to use God—whomever that may be—to facilitate that desire.

The reversal is scarcely an innocent one. The religion of the new rapprochement requires the deity of experiential, subjective religion, a deity that fits neatly into in the modern world, a world that continues to embrace progress as its only real hope.[111] Until recently, that hope was borne almost solely by science and its applications in technology— medical technology in particular. Medicine has—sometimes enthusiastically, sometimes grudgingly, sometimes kicking and screaming in protest—been made the foundation of the modern hope, a hope that subtly suggests that perhaps sickness, pain, and death are not inevitable after all. Now "religion" has been made an ally of medicine in supporting that hope.

Such a hope is from the perspective of the Christian tradition anathema. Yet it is the same Christian tradition, curiously enough, that provides to the modern world the raw material from which the foundation of its hope is constructed: the modern belief in progress is a secularized (and disfigured) version of the Christian hope that God is making all things new.[112] It is to the story of that secularization and its accompanying disfiguration that we turn next.

Christian Reflections
on the Birth of "Religion"

A Downward Spiral toward a Generic Spirituality
and an Instrumentalized Deity

Piety cannot be an instinct craving for a mess of metaphysical and ethical crumbs.

FRIEDRICH SCHLEIERMACHER

It is true . . . that the general course of modern culture has been based on the assumption that the divine is a luxury that cannot be afforded except as it submits to human demands, is totally identified with human knowledge and intention, an aesthetic possibility, or is a domesticated servant of success or self-esteem.

RICHARD E. WENTZ

This chapter and the next require of the reader a certain patience, for we take here a sometimes arduous and convoluted journey in which the destination promised by the introduction and first chapter is often hidden from view. The claim with which we concluded chapter 1 was that the religion of the contemporary rapprochement between medicine and spirituality is at once the product and the servant of the modern hope in un-

limited progress and at the same time a corruption of the Christian eschatological promise. That corruption did not occur because of a conspiracy,
because someone nefarious willed it, or because Christians all at once or
even gradually ceased being faithful. To the contrary, it came about because of the convergence of a constellation of impersonal forces and personal efforts, at least some of which were directed toward the *preservation*
of Christian faithfulness in a world increasingly hostile to Christian commitments. Changes in the way theology was taught in European universities, the rise of modern science and the industrial and technological revo-
lutions, the emergence and eventual ascendancy of the modern liberal
state, and the growth and evolution of capitalist political economy have all
contributed to a fundamental change in the way we have come to think
about notions like "religion" and "spirituality."

It is important to call attention to this, because in this latest stage of
modernity the contemporary mode of thinking about religion and spirituality is very nearly ubiquitous. Therefore it hardly occurs to most of us
to even consider that there might be something wrong with the notion
that religion can be used to make us healthier. The facts bear this out; the
new alliance has plenty of advocates. Its most enthusiastic supporters
within medicine point to the studies indicating that religious people are
healthier than nonreligious people and suggest that caregivers should
consider the use of religion as a therapeutic modality. Meanwhile its advocates among the religious see the same studies, at the very least, as
good public relations—and perhaps as evidence that skeptics may have
new reasons to consider being religious.[1] But, as we suggested in the previous chapter, both of these well-intentioned perspectives miss the mark
theologically.

The most significant *theological* question about the interrelationship of
religion and health is not simply whether being more religious will result
in better health but whether the religion in question, that is, the religion
that ostensibly improves the health of some, teaches its adherents the
sometimes difficult truth about God and God's creation and helps them
live well in and as part of that creation—whether they are sick or well.
And this is not an empirical but a theological question. Theology is concerned with discovering and clarifying what constitutes the boundaries of
an ultimately Good human life, while medicine is concerned to facilitate
the achievement of some of the penultimate goods necessary to achieve
such a life. Just so, questions about the medical utility of a given religion
and the practices constituting that religion have to be considered from
within the boundaries set by that religion's theological tradition, however
permeable and elastic those boundaries may be.

This distinction—between useful religion and religion that tells the truth about God and the world—raises again the question with which we ended chapter 1: Precisely how useful *is* the term "religion," except as a placeholder calling attention to the several (to borrow a term from Wittgenstein) "family resemblances" between otherwise quite divergent sets of beliefs and practices? This might seem a curious and perhaps even an esoteric way of putting the matter to a contemporary North American culture that generally regards religion as personal, private, and very nearly ubiquitous. We have learned to use words like *"religion"* and *"spirituality"* widely and uncritically, to refer to the realm of all things mysterious, unexplainable, or (sometimes) of ultimate importance. "Spirituality" has become an especially popular notion, a word used commonly in everyday speech to refer to our private, individual intercourse with that ineffable "something" beyond the grasp of discursive rationality. The idea that theologians or institutions such as the church should be involved with setting the parameters of that intercourse is especially offensive to our sensibilities.

This is because as moderns, we above all value freedom of conscience in religious matters and assume that reasonable people like us have always felt that way. That kind of sensibility about religion, however, is not simply "there"; it is to a significant extent a product of our particular cultural history.[2] The notion of religious freedom of conscience has at least some of its origins in the Protestant Reformation and the subsequent European wars of religion in the sixteenth and seventeenth centuries. These events did not make "being religious" difficult in the sense that they created widespread popular skepticism about the possibility of belief. Rather, they raised a pointed and at the time urgent political question: "How is society even possible between those of different faiths?"

> Thus, the historical origin of political liberalism (and of liberalism more generally) is the Reformation and its aftermath, with the long controversies over religious toleration in the sixteenth and seventeenth centuries. Something like the modern understanding of liberty of conscience and freedom of thought began then. As Hegel saw, pluralism made religious liberty possible, certainly not Luther's and Calvin's intention.[3]

And this political history is not readily separable from the philosophical and theological history of the same period. The journey from rulers' prudentially offering people the freedom to be Catholic or Protestant, to their permitting and even (in the case of the United States) encouraging them to embrace whichever of the religions they wished, so long as their

belief was relatively suspended in the public sphere, is fairly uncompli-
cated. The further step, in which people came "naturally" to think of religion as "a purely private matter in the sense of an arbitrarily chosen option put together from a copious religious smorgasbord" is not much less
direct.[4] For it is impossible to speak of the origins of freedom of conscience (with respect to religious matters) without at the same time considering the development of the generic notion "religion" and the subsequent devaluation of religious belief as public truth. Only as religion
comes to be understood primarily as the private "intimations of a sub-
limity beyond representation" do questions of truth about what is
believed become subordinate to the individual act of believing.[5] Only as
belief comes to be understood primarily as a universal capacity of
human subjectivity is it possible to talk about "religion" as a genus far
more significant than its many constituent species. And only as "religion"
becomes a category more significant than the great historical traditions
we call "the religions" does a general unwillingness to think or speak
critically with respect to any given object of belief come to characterize
religious discourse.

Precisely these developments took place in Europe, beginning in the
sixteenth and seventeenth centuries. "The construction of the 'genus and
species' model of the relationships between 'the religions' was but one
component," explains Nicholas Lash, "in the project of 'enlightenment.'"[6] Now, we generally assume that the impact of the European Enlightenment on traditional understandings of religion has been primarily
the consequence of the vast knowledge produced by the emergence of
the modern sciences.[7] In the presence of new and highly convincing "scientific" explanations of what was or was not possible, it became untenable for intelligent persons to assent to traditional theological descriptions of everyday physical phenomena, let alone to believe in religious
"miracles" such as resurrection or divine healing.[8] Yet this explanation of
modernity's effect on faith is only partly right. The new explanations of
phenomena produced by the sciences did make belief problematic for
some people. Science's larger impact on religion came about, however,
because of the impact of scientific reasoning on all kinds of *organizing*
knowledge and *speaking* about what was (or could be) known.

Science first helped bring about what moderns know as "religion" because of the success of the scientific method of acquiring knowledge.
The scientific method made careful observation the center of the epis-
temic enterprise, holding that true knowledge was achievable only
through this one method. Thus, "knowledge of nature is arrived at by
looking carefully at the world."[9] Only that which can be seen, touched,

and above all measured can be truly known. Since the object of religious belief falls into none of these categories, theology ceases to be taken seriously as a means of inquiry. It is understood either to be a matter of conjecture about the unseen and immeasurable—what John Milbank calls a "fantasizing about the void"[10]—or one of inductive reason about origins and causes *based on* careful observation of the physical world.[11] "But all this amounts to," Lash reminds us,

> is the claim that the knowledge of God and knowledge of the natural world come about through studying different objects, reading different books: the Scriptures and the "book of nature." In [Sir Francis] Bacon's own words: "though revelation and sense may differ both in matter and manner, yet the spirit of man and its cells are the same; and . . . receive different liquors through different conduits.[12]

And this shift effects a profound change in what it means to be "religious." Since, as Lash remarks, "objects of enquiry are shaped by the methods used for their investigation," the deity who is known through scientific reason is effectively reduced to an object (albeit a very different *kind* of object) that can be subjected to scientific investigation. And since the "scientific" method by which God can be known is by definition universal, then differences of opinion about who or what God is are either the mere temporary remnants of an altogether objectionable parochialism or else reflections of some correctable flaw in the application of the method.

> During the seventeenth century, the terms "theism" and "deism" found their way from France to England and were used, interchangeably for a while, to denote the beliefs of those who affirmed the existence of a Supreme Being, source and author of the world, while rejecting revelation and Christian doctrine. The general deist view was that "pluralism was unnatural, and combined with intolerance, gave rise to untold human misery. The cure was to be a return to the unsullied religion of the *illud tempus* which would result in a universal worship of the one God, and bring an end to religious strife."[13]

Science, moreover, did not serve as a midwife to "religion" by virtue of method only. The knowledges produced by the emergent sciences were accompanied by a significant shift in the way knowledge was organized and represented. Michel Foucault suggests that there was at the end of the sixteenth century a significant disruption in the way people had theretofore thought, spoken, and written about the world.[14] Up until that time, the knowledge of things had been organized largely in terms of their resemblance to one another. Analogy played a significant role in representation, which, Foucault claims, "was posited as a form of repetition: the theatre of life or the mirror of nature, that was the claim made by all language, its manner of declaring its existence and of formulating its right of speech."[15] All things were regarded as part of a "great chain of being"; thus to "search for a meaning is to bring to light a resemblance. To search for the law governing signs is to discover the things that are alike. The grammar of beings is an exegesis of these things."[16]

But with the rise of modernity this way of representation was abandoned, or at least relegated to a decidedly secondary status. The changes effected by the new sciences, by the broad dissemination of printed material, and by the "discovery" of the world beyond Europe produced a quantity of knowledge that demanded for its management a different kind of conceptual apparatus, a new way of thinking and speaking about reality. The new thinking was characterized, says Lash, by two particular characteristics. The first was the conviction that reality, for all its complexity, is fundamentally homogenous. The second characteristic follows closely upon the first: if all reality is fundamentally the same, then the language used to negotiate that reality, in spite of all its richness, is properly univocal.[17]   *language*

> Thus it was that the fusion of the late medieval passion for plain speech and single meanings with the Renaissance rediscovery of Stoicism's "nature"—a world seen as homogenous through and through, made of one kind of stuff and driven by one set of forces—gave birth to a new ideal of the working of the mind, namely: a science that has an unequivocal language with which it speaks and uniform objects of which it speaks. No time nor patience now for narrative, or poetry, or paradox. Theologians, philosophers and scientists alike developed a single-minded passion for pure prose. All knowledge is of objects, and objects are to be measured and described, as objectively and straightforwardly as possible.[18]

The impact of univocal speech on theological discourse was to effect a flattening of that discourse and its subject matter. Theology came to be more about (the possibility of) the willful act of belief than about what had to that time been understood as the proper subject of belief, the particular saving activity of God in history. This effectively "domesticated" the idea of God, making the knowledge of God's existence and attributes finally dependent upon the human intellect and will.[19] The stage was set at the beginning of modernity for the development of a notion of religion that was radically individualized and thus fundamentally susceptible to the calculations of therapeutic self-interest. To the story of that development we now turn.

| | |

A Genealogy of Instrumental Religion: The Turn from Theology to Philosophy

One especially compelling way of telling the story of the birth of a generic, instrumental "religion" begins with Christian theology's abandonment of theology proper. The transformation of inquiry and organization characterizing the sciences was extended to theological discourse, entailing for theology the abandonment of its traditional modes of inquiry and organization, which were determined prior to the seventeenth century by what George Lindbeck has called Christian theology's "regulative principles"[20]—simply another way of saying that the enterprise of Christian theology (not so) gradually abandoned its longstanding insistence that God was to be encountered first and preeminently in the particular narrative history of Israel, Jesus, and the church. And this was a mistake precisely because, as Lash notes,

> We are not incapable, as human beings, of making sense of things, of speaking truth and acting with integrity. But all these things we do from somewhere, shaped by some set of memories and expectations, bearing some sense of duty borne and gifts that have been given. All sense, and truth, and goodness, are carried and constituted by some story, some pattern of experience, some tradition.
>
> Nor are the traditions . . . that we call "religions," an exception to this general rule.[21]

Christian theology's abandonment of its basis in the particular story of Israel, Jesus, and the church was well enough intentioned. It began innocently, with a few subtle changes in the theology curriculum in certain European universities of the seventeenth century, changes that were seen at the time as effective ways to address an increasingly skeptical intellectual climate. The more recent *Summa Theologiae* of Thomas Aquinas replaced the *Sentences* of Peter Lombard, long the cornerstone of theological education in the European universities. More important, the *Summa* was increasingly (and mistakenly) read as a text divisible into relatively independent philosophical and theological treatises.[22]

At the University of Louvain, the chief proponent of this move was the influential Jesuit philosopher Leonard Lessius. Lessius's interests

tended toward law and social ethics; he was persuaded that the o
able basis for an ordered society was a common belief in the existe
God. "To deny the reality of God is to deny that there is any fina.
tion in moral life, a judgment that ultimately allots to each according to
his or her deeds."[23] In his treatise *De Providentia Numinis*, Lessius understood himself to be engaged in a polemic against those who either ignored or denied that the threat of divine judgment was the proper basis
of the social fabric—self-interested politicians and especially atheists.
And because the most notable atheists Lessius encountered were not his
moderately skeptical contemporaries but ancient materialist philosophers such as Democritus, Epicurus, and Lucretius, then "atheism in the
sixteenth and seventeenth centuries is treated as if it were a philosophic
issue, rather than a religious one."[24]

|||

Abandoning Metaphysics: Turning from Philosophy to Natural Science

In short order Lessius's philosophical quest to establish God's existence
became a scientific one. To refute the ancient materialists he turned not
onto Aquinas but also to the Stoics. His reading of the Stoics, and in particular his reading of the works of Cicero, persuaded him that discovering and describing the *order* inhering in the nature of things was fundamental to constructing the foundation on which a viable theology could
be built. Theological arguments were thus reduced to—or at least they
became dependent on—philosophical arguments for the existence of
God. And arguments for the existence of God are all "variations on the
argument from design, from some particular evidence of structure
which demands an intelligence to account for its complex interrelationship. Design is found everywhere."[25] When Lessius read the *Summa Theologiae*, he did so through a Stoic lens, which served not only to reduce
theology to philosophical natural theology but also to place philosophical natural theology on a trajectory that separated it from classical metaphysics, making it instead "derivative by common sense or ordinary
philosophical maxims from astronomy, comparative religion, mechanics,
and biology."[26] Theology was thus in effect made the province of the sciences. And nowhere was the project of arguing derivatively from the
order of nature in defense of God taken up more vigorously than in the
work of Sir Isaac Newton.[27]

Newton's great concern was mechanics, the movement of objects in
space. His interest in the apparent regularities of all repetitive motion,

whether of objects in the laboratory or of the celestial bodies, led him to search for ways to "derive absolute and true mathematical motion, with its space and time."[28] For Newton this was a theological quest as well as a scientific one, precisely because it was comprehensive: "Newton wrote a mechanics of the world that explained the world as a mechanical system. This ineluctably raised questions about the one whom Newton called 'the Author of the system.'"[29]

Newton's "theological" project was thus an outgrowth of his work in mechanics, in which he aimed ultimately at the mathematical derivation of what Buckley calls "absolute" space and time. His work proceeds, Buckley explains, by a method of analysis and synthesis. Precisely this method enabled Newton to entertain theological questions in the same work in which he was calculating the laws of motion. In Newton's *Principia,*

> Analysis is the resolution of effects into their causes, whether one is dealing with the solution of compounds into ingredients or of movements into their diverse and originating forces. Analysis is not a movement simply into particularities. It begins with particularity and it moves to particular causes; but it continues this causal resolution until it uncovers the general laws which are the reason these particular causes act in this particular way.
>
> Synthesis moves in precisely the opposite manner: from cause to effect. Granted the general laws of mass, distance and force; granted further these particular forces inherent in this body and impressed by the agency of other influences; synthesis describes the career they will effect.[30]

Now, this project seems destined to have taken on an explicitly theological aspect. Intellectuals in England at the beginning of the eighteenth century were as concerned with religion as with science, and many of the great scientists were people of faith who saw their work as contributing to, rather than compromising, belief. Whereas the scholars of mechanics on the European continent—who had inherited Descartes's rationalist assertion that the material world had nothing to do with God—tended to be materialists "all the way down," so to speak, the British mechanists who followed Newton saw their work as a kind of participation in the work of God.[31] Newton had offered an account of the movement of the entire solar system, and that account had posed, explains Buckley, an obvious question: "What lies at the origin of its compound movements?" It was a simple question of causes.

The intelligibility of a compound movement is found through analytic resolution into its causes; these causes or forces are generalized through induction. Newtonian mechanics never maintained that mechanics had to reduce everything to *mechanical* causes. It did demand a *coherence of procedure*, that one should not cut off the analytic method arbitrarily through hypotheses. In fact, for Newton, these two inconsistencies coalesce: the arbitrary termination of analysis and synthesis and the elaboration of simple mechanical causes. The only way that one can arbitrarily terminate the process of mechanical analysis is by fabricating a gratuitous mechanical cause. Newton understood this to be the cardinal sin of Cartesian mechanics.[32]

In place of (what he believed was) the strictly hypothetical mechanical first cause of the Cartesians, Newton maintained that natural philosophy ought to proceed by deducing causes from effects "till we come to the very first Cause, which certainly is not Mechanical."[33] Newton determined the first cause was a personal agent who was "well skilled in Mathematics and Geometry." He arrived at this conclusion not simply because he brought to his work a prior belief in a personal God but also because the existence of such an agent was the logical outcome of his method. In Buckley's words: "How is it possible to talk about true, absolute, and mathematical motion and not be doing theology?"[34]

But a God whose existence and attributes are known only, or even first, in the regular operations of the natural world is also dependent on being the only or at least the best explanation for those operations.[35] Newton had assumed, based on his experiments and calculations, that the compound movements of the solar system had to have a simple first cause. And he assumed this cause had to be personal, rather than mechanical, because it was untenable, given the science of the day, to argue that matter initiated, sustained, or regulated its own movement. So just to the extent that theologians embraced Newton's arguments, they made the intelligibility of their discourse dependent on the scientific viability of those arguments.

For a time, Newton's universal mechanics did remain viable. At the middle of the eighteenth century, most intellectuals seem to have assumed that Newton had gotten it right; the world had quite obviously been made and set in motion by an intelligent designer, and the regularity of the celestial orbits, among other things, was proof of this. In the generation after Newton, the leading exponent and then interlocutor of Newton's system was the French philosopher Denis Diderot.

Early in his career, Diderot was a convinced deist. The increasing influence of Newton, Descartes, and others led him to develop a religious epistemology that was a sort of dialectic between experience and reason. Experience, no matter how sublime, was by itself an inadequate foundation for religious belief:

> The eruptions of temperament tell us nothing about the nature of god [*sic*]; in fact, that god they fabricate is often a monster. His irrational rages, the implacable vengeance he wreaks on human beings, the *massa dominata* of Augustinian theology—these notions, which rot at the heart of superstition, tempt the upright to wish for a godless reality and drive others from skepticism to atheism. An ultimate paradox rules the absolute reliance upon religious experiences and passions: Such a religious attitude moves through superstition and skepticism and finally terminates in atheism.[36]

Just so, religious experience and the human response to that experience—"temperament"—needed to be tried and tempered by the canons of scientific reason. If there was a God, Diderot maintained, then there had to be evidence for that God's existence. That evidence existed either in the transcendent reality of human reason, as Descartes had argued, or in the order inherent in the physical universe, as Newton had claimed. Diderot considered and then rejected Descartes, believing that the Cartesian method ultimately ended in skepticism.[37] That rejection placed the entire burden of proof of God's existence on the order discernible in the physical universe:

> Religious experience leads to superstition, which leads to atheism. Metaphysics leads to contradicting systems, which lead to skepticism. Experimental physics, in contrast, leads to the "true knowledge of nature," which leads to deism. Nature, not experience or speculative ideas, constitutes the only evidence in the universe that can support theistic commitments. Diderot's *Pensees* exhibit in miniature the development of natural theology since the days of Lessius and Mersenne. Theology gives way to Cartesianism, which gives way to Newtonian mechanics. The great argument, the only evidence for theism, is design, and experimental physics reveals that design.[38]

Experimental physics revealed design because the regularities of movement that could be observed and calculated presume the existence of an intelligence that had initiated and ordered those patterns. But what if another, more tenable, explanation for these regularities was to emerge? What then of God? The Newtonian deists were soon forced to engage just such an explanation.

The newly developed discipline of mathematical probability suggested that the universe, orderly as it seemed to be, could possibly have come about by chance. "If one grants that matter has been eternally in movement, and that the multitude of atoms is infinite, and that the possible combinations that would compose a system are infinite, there is nothing so strange in the possibility that one of these combinations has occurred."[39] Diderot conceded this point, understanding that it required a revision of the Newtonian system. The revision he offered initially was to turn away from structure—that is, from Newtonian mechanical design—and to focus instead on what Buckley calls "an organic purposiveness that needs to be explained."[40] Diderot thought such a teleological reorientation of the argument from design could stand up to the canons of mathematical probability. "Diderot's *Pensees* are . . . a coordinate search for principle, first in the physical universe and then in the reflective, scientific intellect. In both cases, the principle is reflexive. . . . But what if that principle should change?"[41]

| | |

The Argument Backfires: God Becomes an "Unnecessary" Hypothesis

In Diderot's *Pensees*, God's existence was arguable on the basis of the purposeful order present in the organic world.[42] But certain readers of that work, chief among them Nicholas Saunderson, professor of mathematics at Cambridge, dissented from Diderot's conclusions. Saunderson followed Diderot's own method to engage the Newtonian argument on its own terms and saw no need to invoke God as being at the origin.[43] For Saunderson believed that Newton and his deist followers had never taken seriously arguments that had in one form or another existed from the first century, arguments for a randomly originating, yet now ordered, universe: "La matiere se mouvoir et le chaos se debrouiller."[44]

> If we were to go back to the origin of things and the beginnings of time, what would we perceive? Precisely what Descartes has suggested in his mechanics: matter in motion. But in this scenario there is no need for god [*sic*] to establish matter and the laws of nature. Descartes only goes halfway, artificially deriving his mechanics from the divine attributes. Saunderson's real master is Titus Lucretius

Carus. Newton's natural theology is to be refuted by the hypothesis drawn from the great Epicurean poet.[45]

Matter spontaneously achieving order through motion thus became the guiding principle for the scientific worldview. And theology, having agreed some time before that science was the proper forum for considering the question of God, was for at least a time left unable to answer—except by claiming that conclusive proof of God's existence was as near as the next stage of development in experimental physics, which would surely disprove this principle.[46] But that development never materialized. The natural theology of Newton, in the hands of Diderot, Saunderson, and those who followed them, culminated in the philosophical atheism of men like Condillac and d'Holbach.[47]

By making itself dependent on natural philosophy and then on physical and biological science, theology abandoned its traditional position, that God was to be encountered first of all in the narrative history of Israel, Jesus, and the church and that the world was to be understood fully only as it was taken up into and enveloped by that history. When the sciences arrived late in the eighteenth century at the apparent terminus of an inherently atheist materialism, announcing that if God existed, there was certainly scant evidence for that existence in nature, theology was forced to find a new ground on which to meet with God. That new meeting-place was human consciousness. Its soil, fertilized by the rotting corpse of deist natural theology, proved a hospitable medium for the cultivation of the notion "religion" and its contemporary partner, "spirituality."

III

The Turn to "Religion": Reclaiming a Space for God

Certain aspects of the religious turn to the subject preceded the end of the eighteenth century. A "politics of privatization" had played a steadily increasing role in religious discourse since the Reformation; the developments at the end of the eighteenth and beginning of the nineteenth century only served to consolidate that role. As the "scientific" natural religion of the Enlightenment found itself increasingly at odds with the science of the day, it came also to be assumed that religion could not be about truth, at least not in the same sense that science is about truth.[48] Rather, religion came to be understood as having to do with the deepest matters of the human heart, with "private feelings, hermetic practices, individual and tribal fantasies, which was first called 'positive' religion and then, in due course, tended to be referred to simply as 'religion' *tout court*."[49]

This is not to say that the religious turn to the subject transpired without intellectual support; far from it. One of its most widely accepted bases was provided by the great German philosopher Immanuel Kant, who declared in his *Critique of Pure Reason* the advent of a new Copernican revolution in philosophy.[50] Kant was no stranger to the natural sciences. He knew and understood Newton, but he argued that Newton made a category mistake in claiming that knowledge of the order inherent in the physical universe led to knowledge of God.[51] For Kant, all attempts to offer metaphysical proofs of God's existence are problematic. Buckley explains:

> The natural theologies always collapse because their reach exceeds their grasp, because they attempt to employ pure concepts beyond the manifold of experience. Unlike mathematics and physics, metaphysics in its prior forms—openly in the Universal Mathematics of Descartes, or even disguised in the Universal Mechanics of Newton—removes its concepts from their necessary connection with sensuous intuition, and it reaches not what can be known but only what can be thought.[52]

This is not to say that Kant believed that philosophical argument could not be marshaled in support of evidence for God's existence. Although he believed that metaphysical proofs for the existence of God were specious, he did hold that the existence of the human sense of duty, which he called the "moral law within," was made possible by the existence of God. God, in other words, was a "necessary postulate of the human ethical life."[53] For Kant, the evidence for God's existence lay neither in the abstractions of the Cartesian *cogito* nor in the order of the Newtonian physical world but in the moral sensibilities written on the heart of every rational person. So although he was considerably skeptical toward the historical claims of particular "ecclesiastical faiths," Kant was a great defender of religion, which he said "is hidden within and has to do with moral dispositions."[54]

Considered in itself, the philosophical project that begins with Lessius and winds its way to Kant appears to be quite removed from the concerns of this book. Yet we dare not underestimate the influence of that project on religious belief and practice, first among Protestant Christians and then among religious people more generally, in the generations following Kant up to the present. An increasing majority of theologians assumed, in one way or another, that Kant was correct in his insistence that religion is properly a matter of some aspect of inward human subjectivity. In spite of their sometimes considerable differences with Kant, the theologians of the nineteenth century all agreed "on one particular point in relation to all the particular world views of their time: man's supposedly innate and essential capacity to 'sense and taste the infinite.'"[55]

| | |

Scheliermacher and the Turn to Feeling

Friedrich Schleiermacher is widely regarded as the seminal figure in the development of modern religious consciousness. Schleiermacher was initially educated by Moravians at Breslau and then studied theology and philosophy at Halle. By 1796, he was pastor of a large church in Berlin; it was here that he became an active participant in that city's intellectual salon culture. He found himself frequently confronted by a general disinterest in or disdain for religion among his sophisticated contemporaries.[56] In response, and as an initial articulation of his own theological position, he wrote his now famous treatise *On Religion: Speeches to its Cultured Despisers*. Karl Barth has said of the *Speeches*: "Whoever wishes to know and understand this [nineteenth-century] theology must read this little book with great care, though it is by no means easily digested."[57] Our concerns diverge somewhat from Barth's, but his point is nonetheless salient. For contemporary "religion" has been deeply influenced by Schleiermacher, and one can scarcely understand contemporary religious consciousness without understanding Schleiermacher's *Speeches*.

At the root of Schleiermacher's work in the *Speeches,* and later in his systematic work *The Christian Faith* (*Die Glaubenslehre*), is a simultaneous embrace and rejection of Kant. That is, Schleiermacher went along with Kant's argument that religion began with and was fundamentally a matter of interior human subjectivity, yet he departed from Kant by arguing that religion was not, as Kant had maintained, reducible to an innate moral sensibility. Religion was irreducible and was concerned above all with the one universal human attribute: feeling.[58]

Schleiermacher's understanding of religion centers on this absolute conviction: that human subjectivity is always and everywhere irreducibly and universally religious. He saw neither the existence of a plurality of religious beliefs nor the apparent atheism of some as refuting this conviction. For these were merely corruptions of the "original, characteristic form" of religion, which "is not accustomed to appear openly, but is only seen in secret by those who love it."[59] Those who failed to find intellectual justification for believing were in Schleiermacher's mind merely looking in the wrong places. They needed to look in the realm of feeling, "Wherefore every activity of the spirit is to be understood, in so far as a man can study it in himself."[60]

This is not to say that Schleiermacher denied absolutely that religion was manifest in the realms of thought or action. He simply thought it was a mistake to look in either of those places for the essence of religion, which existed in a realm seldom investigated in the sophisticated modern world:

> Among ourselves at the present time this is specially recognized. It belongs to the opposition of the new time to the old that no longer is one person one thing, but everyone is all things. Just as among civilized peoples, by extensive intercourse their characteristic ways of thought no longer appear unalloyed, so in the human mind there is such a complete sociableness founded, that no special faculty or capacity, however much it be separated for observation, can ever, in separation, produce its work. Speaking broadly, one is, in operation, influenced and permeated by the ready love and support of the others. The predominating power is all you can distinguish.[61]

Essential religion is thus reducible neither to ethics, as Kant maintained, nor to physics and metaphysics, as the deists had argued. Although religion "never appears quite pure" and its "outward form is ever determined by something else," it exists in an ideal sense as itself alone.[62] Consequently, true religion "resigns, at once, all claims on anything that belongs either to science or morality," for it is ultimately concerned with something else entirely, nor does it need to make a case for itself.[63]

The purest manifestation of the essence of religion, said Schleiermacher, was not in action or analysis but in the contemplation of that which is beyond the realms of action and analysis. "The contemplation of the pious," he said, "is the immediate consciousness of the universal existence of all finite things, in and through the Infinite, and of all temporal things in and through the Eternal."[64] Thus, religion has to do with that which is *beyond* both science and ethics, in the sense that it is the immediate intuition of that greater "something," which both science and ethics allude to but fail to address. "True science is complete vision; true practice is culture and art self-produced; true religion is sense and taste for the Infinite."[65] Neither science nor practice can exist in their "true" states independent of religion. For neither can "come to life in you except in so far as there lives immediately in you the external unity of Reason and Nature, the universal existence of all finite things in the Infinite."[66] The point at which finitude confronts and considers its opposite—which is also its fulfillment—that is where religion is to be found.

It is the first contact of the universal life with an individual. It fills no time and fashions nothing palpable. It is the holy wedlock of the Universe with the incarnated Reason for a creative, productive embrace. It is immediate, raised above all error and misunderstanding. You lie directly on the bosom of the infinite world.[67]

Having made this initial claim about what the essence of religion is, Schleiermacher's next task is to describe precisely where and how this intuition of the infinite transpires. Human consciousness, he argues, consists in three interdependent faculties: perception, feeling, and activity.

Take what belongs to each class and consider it by itself. You will find that those moments in which you exercise power over things and impress yourselves upon them, form what you call your practical, or in a narrower sense, your moral life; again the contemplative moments, be they few or many, in which things produce themselves in you as intuition, you will doubtless call the scientific life. Now can either series alone form a human life? Would it not be death? If each activity were not stimulated and renewed by the other, would it not be self-consumed? Yet they are not identical. If you would understand your life and speak comprehensibly of it, they must be distinguished. As it stands with these two in respect of one another, it must stand with the third in respect of both. How then are you to name this third, which is the series of feeling? What life will it form? The religious as I think, and as you will not be able to deny, when you have considered it more closely.[68]

Religion is what transpires in the realm of feeling, at least insofar as feeling is directed beyond the particular toward the universal, beyond the finite to the Infinite.[69] And because the Infinite makes itself present through and as the fulfillment of and the opposite of the finite, all feelings are potentially constitutive of religion, indications that the Infinite is acting upon and within the individual.[70] They need only come from within the individual and be "indubitably your own feelings, and not mere stale descriptions of the feelings of others, which could at best issue in a wretched imitation."[71]

On this point, Schleiermacher is adamant; even though the development and promulgation of religious myths and dogmas and then of theories of religion is inevitable, none of these should be confused with religion proper. True religion, which is the source of all religious myth, dogma, and theory, is finally beyond criticism, so long as it meets one criterion. "The sum total of religion is to feel that, in its highest unity, all that moves us in feeling is one; to feel that aught single and particular is only possible by means of this unity; to feel, that is to say, that our being and living is a being and living through God."[72]

And who or what is God in Schleiermacher's account of religion? At least formally, we can say that for Schleiermacher God is whatever might be the final cause of or ultimate reason for all human feeling. Defining God in this way is a critical move for Schleiermacher, in that it dictates that he take a particular attitude not simply toward "religion" proper (i.e., toward the "essence" of religion) but also toward any particular religious tradition. His move to justify religion by locating it solely in the realm of human feeling leads him toward a peculiar kind of irenical skepticism toward historical religious traditions. "It is not necessary," he remarks, "that the Deity be presented as . . . one distinct object." Some may choose to represent God in this way, but they should not be drawn into thinking theirs is the only proper representation of the cause of feelings; in fact, they should be aware of the dangers inherent in that representation.[73]

> That the religious sense of one person is moved in one way, and that of another in another is not pure accident, as if the emotions formed no whole, as if any emotions might be caused in the same individual by the same object. Whatever occurs anywhere, whether among many or few as a peculiar and distinct kind of feeling is in itself complete, and by its nature necessary. What you find as religious emotions among Turks or Indians, cannot equally appear among Christians. The essential oneness of religiousness spreads itself out in a great variety of provinces, and again, in each province it contracts itself, and the narrower and smaller the province there is necessarily more excluded as incompatible and more included as characteristic. . . . Religion thus fashions itself with endless variety, down even to the single personality.[74]

Schleiermacher therefore manages the deist problem of religious pluralism not by disparaging it as superstition but by embracing it. Pure religion will manifest itself in a variety of ways purely as a matter of course, since representations of religion always and everywhere occur only at the intersection of feeling (which is universal) with contingency. For finite beings, it could not be otherwise. God is not the one represented in this or that doctrinal or ritual manifestation of religious feeling but the universal final cause of the feelings themselves.[75] This is in Schleiermacher's mind obvious and requires only a bit of reflection: the goal of the religious person should be finally to transcend his or her particular representation of religion. "In every species of religious feeling he will then become conscious of all that lies beyond the department which he directly cultivates."[76] Such consciousness thus becomes an "immediate consciousness of the Deity as He is found in ourselves and in the world."[77]

Schleiermacher is obviously walking a tightrope on this point. On the one hand, he is decidedly critical of those notions of God he understands typically to be held by the adherents of the Abrahamic religions. He calls this the classical or "usual conception of God as one single being outside of the world and behind the world."[78] On the other hand, however, he does not intend simply to make of God a cipher for a particular aspect of human consciousness. God clearly exists for Schleiermacher as more than just a product of an autonomous human consciousness; there is still room here for religion to play something like a prophetic role. In the introductory chapter of his *Christian Faith*, which is perhaps more representative of his mature thought, than the *Speeches* , he maintains that "in every self-consciousness there are two elements, which we might call respectively a self-caused element . . . and a non-self-caused element . . . ; or a Being and a Having-by-some-means-come-to-be." Self-consciousness has a cause that is beyond itself, "another factor besides the Ego, a factor which is the source of the particular determination, and without which the self consciousness would not be precisely what it is."[79]

This is to say that for Schleiermacher, feeling is theologically significant precisely because it is *not* completely self-originating. The entirety of human feeling is produced by a *series* of causes. The "non-self-caused element" of feeling, that which has its origin beyond the subject in an Other or others, he calls the feeling of dependence. The "self-caused element" of feeling, on the other hand, having its origin within the subject, he calls the feeling of freedom. Individuals are aware—they *feel*—upon reflection, that they have become the persons they are by virtue of the entire, reciprocal work of a cluster of feeling-engendering forces, some of which are not self-originating.[80] "Accordingly our self-consciousness, as a consciousness of our existence in the world or of our co-existence with the world, is a series in which the feeling of freedom and the feeling of dependence are divided."[81]

Now, neither of these aspects of consciousness can be absolute insofar as they constitute the self-consciousness of any one individual. Moreover, the feeling of freedom can never be absolute, for that feeling always finds its expression in a free action upon or toward an object—an other—and such an object is always given to the subject from without.[82] This means that every feeling of freedom is accompanied by a feeling of dependence on some other. The existence of that feeling, moreover, is at least partly independent of the agent's free activity toward it. Ultimately, every agent discovers that he or she is inescapably dependent.

Every feeling of freedom arising from a free act is thus accompanied by a feeling of dependence on the object of that act. Now in itself, any instance of such a feeling of dependence is relative, since the object causing that one instance of feeling depends on that object's contingent presence. In this sense the feeling of dependence is as relative as the feeling of freedom; "For every moment which is made up of a partial feeling of freedom and a partial feeling of dependence places us in a position of co-ordinate antithesis to a similar Other."[83] In a broader sense, however, the feeling of dependence is absolute, because consciousness, which seems to be constant (i.e., absolute), is never *not* dependent on some object.[84] Consciousness is always consciousness *of* something; in recognizing these objects of consciousness as finite and dependent, we also recognize our selves as finite and so as *absolutely* dependent. Therefore:

> The highest self-consciousness is in no wise dependent on outwardly given objects which may affect us at one moment and not at another. As a consciousness of absolute dependence it is quite simple, and remains self-identical while all other states are changing. Therefore, in itself it cannot possibly be at one moment thus and at another moment otherwise, nor can it by intermission be present at one moment and absent at another. Either it is not there at all, or, so long as it is there, it is continuously there and always self-identical.[85]

Schleiermacher thus defends the central proposition of his philosophy of religion, that the "self-identical essence of piety is this: the consciousness of being absolutely dependent, or, which is the same thing, of being in relation with God."[86]

One would think that Schleiermacher's subjectivism would mean that his account of religion is completely uncritical with respect to content, but this is not the case. In fact, he thinks it is quite important to elaborate the most appropriate form of belief; he has a good deal to say about the proper object of absolute dependence. Because religious self-consciousness is an "essential element of human nature," the development of human communities that are centered around that consciousness is to be expected. "Fellowship," he explains, "is demanded by the *consciousness of kind* which dwells in every man, and which finds its satisfaction only when he steps forth beyond the limits of his own personality and takes up the facts of other personalities into his own."[87]

In actuality, religious practice will not be completely homogenous, for there will always be differences in religious consciousness among the members of a given community, not to mention differences between communities. Such differences are based largely on the extent to which those members and their communities "distinguish the religious content of [their] self-consciousness from the sensible to which it is related."[88] In spite of these differences, however, there will be a tendency to move toward homogeneity both within and among communities as religious consciousness develops through its several stages. Such development relates closely both to the evolution of cultural forms and the development of mental powers, such that Schleiermacher indicates that advanced cultures will show a proclivity for an increasingly abstract monotheism, while less sophisticated cultures will tend toward "idol worship."[89] He thus continues to identify himself as a Christian and to insist on the relative superiority of Christianity, not because he is persuaded that the Christian story truthfully narrates the history of the world but because he believes that Christianity is better suited than other religious traditions to being expressed as the consciousness of absolute dependence.

Schleiermacher's work is significant for the argument we are developing here because that work represents a crucial step toward the legitimization of the placing of divinity in the service of human agency. Schleiermacher's work serves to solidify the broad consensus, first among Protestant Christians and then throughout European and North American culture, that whenever someone speaks about religion or spirituality, they are talking about basically the same thing, namely, a basic, universal aspect of human consciousness reflecting a set of basic, universal human needs. This is not to say that Schleiermacher himself understood religion as entirely self-serving and therapeutic. Karl Barth says it is an "injustice to Schleiermacher (and his followers right up to our own day) is we foist upon them the intention . . . of making the human subject the creator of his determination by God, as though their theology were direct Cartesianism."[90] Yet the fact remains that Schleiermacher's account of religion is radically subjective and highly individualized. Abstracted from any potentially countercultural narration of history, such a religion is ineluctably bound to the dominant culture and thus dependent for its viability *on* that culture. In a culture that privileges the individual and values the therapeutic, the religion will tend always to be subjective and therapeutic.

| | |

Feuerbach Takes the Next Step

Those who most clearly foresaw this possibility in the generations after Schleiermacher were the so-called left Hegelians, especially Ludwig Feuerbach and Karl Marx. Hegel, the predecessor of both Marx and Feuerbach, was Schleiermacher's contemporary. His thought represented the primary early nineteenth-century theological alternative to that of Schleiermacher—at least to the extent that Hegel's thought can legitimately be called theological; for, as Alasdair MacIntyre reminds us, "Hegel's concern from the outset is with history, not with theology, but . . . he approaches history with categories drawn from a religious background."[91]

Hegel believed that Christianity, although not true on its own terms, nevertheless provided a "clue to the nature of man's ultimate redemption,"[92] which consisted in the human journey in history from alienation to objectification to coming to one's own.[93] For Hegel, the ultimate universal (hence the sole human) telos was freedom. He saw history as "a path from unfreedom to freedom," a progressive realization of the fact that all humans, in spite of historical circumstances that would indicate otherwise, are essentially equal and hence equally free.[94] In the end, Hegel believed, religion would be completely interiorized. Christianity pointed in this direction, recognizing something of the human potential for freedom, but ultimately failed because it remained, as do all religions, dependent on symbol and narrative.

> The Christian doctrine of God incarnate in Jesus symbolizes for Hegel the ultimate unity of man and God, of finite and infinite Spirit. But because religion is a product of man's estrangement it objectifies its symbols, it makes God-man hood the attribute of one particular being at one particular place, and so becomes superstition. Reason must therefore oppose religion, which falls before its [reason's] attacks—Hegel is here thinking of eighteenth-century rationalism; but at the critical point philosophy shows the inner truth of what religion has been trying to say.[95]

Hegel's understanding of history and human freedom were significant influences on the thought of Ludwig Feuerbach, who took up Hegel's project but rejected its idealism, its flight to abstraction. Feuerbach was a materialist, and his materialism meant that he was unwilling to dispense with religion as quickly as was Hegel; he sought instead to explain it. At this point, he became indebted to Schleiermacher. According to Van Harvey, Feuerbach's thought depends on two methodological rules, which represent his "attempt to reconcile the different postures that Hegel and Schleiermacher took to religion."

The first of these is that since religion is humanity's "earliest and indirect form of self-knowledge," the most immediate and earliest expressions of the religious consciousness should be taken as the most revelatory and authentic. The second rule is that "the nearer religion stands to its origin, the truer, the more genuine it is, the less its nature is disguised because in the origin of religion there is no *qualitative* or *essential* distinction between God and man. And the religious man is not shocked at this identification."[96]

Clearly, then, Feuerbach did not believe that Schleiermacher had gotten religion right. Like Schleiermacher, he understood feeling to be the basis of religion; he "insisted that the religious utterances of the religious consciousness are revelatory of feeling."[97] Yet he also understood that Schleiermacher's evocation of the "non-self-caused element" of feeling that leads to the feeling of absolute dependence on God was finally arbitrary. And this suspicion concerning the arbitrariness of Schleiermacher's insistence that the feeling of dependence validated belief in the Christian God led Feuerbach to adopt a critical posture toward religion in general and the Christian faith in particular.

That critical posture—especially as it pertains to our project—can be summed up by saying that Feuerbach believed that religion was always and everywhere the product of the projection of certain fundamental human attributes and desires, resulting in the human creation of an imaginary, mythic being called "God."[98] As Feuerbach says at the beginning of the third of his *Lectures on the Essence of Religion*, "Theology is anthropology."[99]

A God is essentially a being who fulfills man's desires. And the most heartfelt desire, at least *of those* men whose desires are not curtailed by natural necessity, is the desire not to die, to live forever; this is indeed man's highest and ultimate desire, the desire of all desires just as life is the epitome of all blessings for that very reason.[100]

But this does not mean that Feuerbach's view of religion was negative, at least not after the fashion of the scientific materialists of the eighteenth century, who viewed religion as malignant and sought to abolish it. John Milbank rightly says, it is "more helpful to view Feuerbach's work, not as a stage in a long story of retreat [from belief], but rather as another example of the nineteenth century post-Enlightenment reaction *in favour* of religion, albeit in this case in the form of a search for a 'religion of humanity.'"[101] According to Milbank, "Feuerbach's goal was precisely to exhibit man as truly and in essence the subject of the divine predicates, the worthy object of worship."[102] And this claim is borne out by Feuerbach's writing on religion, which, in spite of the fact that it begins with an account of man, is itself deeply religious.

"Religion," Feuerbach writes in his most widely read work, *The Essence of Christianity*, "has its basis in the essential difference between man and the brute—the brute has no religion."[103] The one characteristic separating humans from other creatures is that humans alone are conscious of themselves as a species. That is, humans have the ability to think about themselves as humans. A person who has this ability, says Feuerbach, can "put himself in the place of another." And it is precisely this capacity that gives to humans the ability to be religious: "Religion being identical with the distinctive characteristic of man, is then identical with self-consciousness—with the consciousness which man has of his nature."[104]

That nature, Feuerbach goes on to claim, consists in three aspects. Humans possess reason, will, and affection. These are "absolute perfections of being," for humans exist "to think, to love, to will," and these for their own sake: "True existence is thinking, loving, willing existence."[105] Religion is nothing other than the ideation of those perfections that constitute the human essence. Thus, Feuerbach explains, "so far as thy nature reaches, so far reaches thy unlimited self-consciousness, so far art thou God."[106] Here Feuerbach most closely resembles Schleiermacher; he suggests that just to the extent that humans are self-conscious, they are also religious.[107] "The mystery of the inexhaustible fulness [*sic*] of the divine predicates is therefore nothing else than the mystery of human nature considered as an infinitely varied, infinitely modifiable, but, consequently, phenomenal being."[108] Religion, properly understood, is simply a full consideration of the nearly limitless possibilities afforded by human being.

The problem, according to Feuerbach, is that religion is seldom properly understood. Humans fail to grasp the possibilities offered by their "true" natures and instead project those possibilities onto an imagined, "perfect" god. "To enrich God, man must become poor; that God may be all, man must be nothing. . . . What man withdraws from himself, what he renounces in himself, he only enjoys in as incomparably higher and fuller measure in God."[109] And this is an unhappy occurrence because it requires that women and men deny or at least distort their own true natures as thinking, loving, and willing beings. This is for Feuerbach the "mystery" of religion: "Man . . . projects his being into objectivity, and then again makes himself an object to this projected image of himself thus converted into a subject; he thinks of himself is [*sic*] an object to himself, but as the object of an object, of another being than himself. Thus here. Man is an object to God."[110]

This act of projection by which humans create an objective God and are alienated from their true selves (it is in his flirtations with this notion of alienation that the Hegelian influence on Feuerbach is most evident) happens because humans, in spite of their potential for greatness, are consumed by intractable and all too earthly desires. To put it a bit too starkly, we want things we do not have, and we can neither satisfy nor escape those wants. Therefore through an act of the imagination we create an ideal being who has those things we want and that, we believe, might offer some of them to us in exchange for our adoration.

> Man believes in gods not only because he has imagination and feeling, but also because he has the striving to be happy. He believes in the existence of happy beings, not only because he has a conception of happiness, but because he himself wishes to be happy; he believes in a perfect being because he himself wishes to be perfect; he believes in an immortal being because he himself does not wish to die. What he himself is not but would like to be, he conceives of as existing in his gods; the gods are men's desires conceived as realities, transformed into real beings. A god is man's striving for happiness, fulfilled in his imagination. For all man's imagination and feeling, he would have no gods if he had no desires.[111]

Here Feuerbach follows Schleiermacher—up to a point. He says with Schleiermacher that "the foundation of religion is the feeling of dependency; the first object of that feeling is nature; thus nature is the first object of religion."[112] Because humanity has for a long time been subject to, and in a very fundamental way dependent on, nature for its existence, humans have worshiped nature—or perhaps it would be better to say they worshiped the *forces* of nature—as God. Thus humans have developed a ritualized set of practices the aim of which is to placate the gods and goddesses of nature and get from them those things most immediately required for human existence. Over time, however, humans have begun to imagine themselves capable of mastering nature. Just to the extent that they have achieved that mastery, nature has ceased to be an object of worship. Consequently the pantheon of pagan gods and goddesses, whom Feuerbach insists owed their existence to a kind of vulgar utility with respect to the forces of nature, have been abandoned in favor of a more anthropomorphic God whose concern for human happiness is more profound and unconditional.[113] This, says Feuerbach, is the God of the Abrahamic religions and especially of Christianity.[114]

The God of Christianity—at least as Feuebach understands Christianity—is humanity's "true *alter ego*."[115] As such, this God is concerned to satisfy the deepest, most complex human longings. Faith in this God is faith in the possibility of the impossible, faith in a God who has power over those several forces that (in God's absence) invariably frustrate human desire. "Thus the belief in God and the belief in miracles are one: the only difference between miracle and God is the difference between action and agent."[116] Prayer to such a God, claimed Feuerbach, represents the vocalization of the deepest human longings, the subordination of nature to individual human desires and needs.[117] Prayer is thus the truest expression of the egoism that is fundamentally constitutive of human being.[118] It is "the self-division of man into two beings—a dialogue of man with himself, with his heart."[119]

Finally, Feuerbach indicates, prayer and the belief in miracles are reducible to expressions of the ultimate human desire, the desire not to die. He called this desire the "rage to live," or *Gluckseligkeitstrieb*, and regarded it as "the most important subjective feature driving religious belief . . . the Promethean desire to be free from all evils, from the oppression of matter, from death, and from the limitations of nature."[120] This ultimate desire, he argues, is represented by Christian mythology's ultimate miracle, the resurrection of Christ from the dead; it is by believing that Christ has been raised from the dead that the basic human desire not to die is satisfied. For the wish not to die, he explains,

> involves the further wish for the certainty of its fulfillment. Reason can afford no such certainty. It has therefore said that all proofs of immortality are insufficient, and even that unassisted reason is not capable of apprehending it, still less of proving it. And with justice; for reason furnishes only general proofs; it cannot give the certainty of any personal immortality, and it is precisely this certainty which is desired. Such a certainty requires an immediate personal assurance, a practical demonstration. This can only be given to me by the fact of a dead person, whose death has been previously certified, rising again from the grave; and he must be no indifferent person, but, on the contrary, the type and representative of all others, so that his resur-

rection also may be the type, the guarantee of theirs. The resurrection of Christ is therefore the satisfied desire of man for an immediate certainty of his personal existence after death—personal immortality as a sensible, indubitable fact.[121]

Feuerbach did not actually believe that Christ was risen from the dead, nor did he believe in the possibility of human immortality in the sense of life without temporal end. He did, however, believe that these religious ideas were important clues to the truth about human nature and its possibilities. And it is precisely here that his work stands as a remarkable predictor of the dominant religion of contemporary North America, the religion embraced by the advocates of the contemporary rapprochement between religion and medicine. This is not to say that Feuerbach would necessarily have approved of that religion, but he certainly would have understood it. For the religion of the contemporary rapprochement can be largely explained by narrating the intersection of the anthropocentric religion of the nineteenth century with the forces of late capitalist modernity. We now turn to an account of that intersection.

Religious Belief as Commodity Fetishism
Individualism, Therapy, and the Market

*Lacking the courage, the tranquility, the self-knowledge to find our freedom
here, we flee. Our flight takes one of two forms. The first is the flight into feeling, on the run from darkness, inhumanity and impending chaos. Whatever
we make of William James' claim that drunkenness stands, "to the poor and
unlettered . . . in the place of symphony concerts and of literature" (a
claim that bites both ways), it would be difficult to deny that the upsurge of
"religiousness" in Western culture, of piety peddled as balm for frightened
and alienated subjectivity, suggests that narcotic uses of religion are still as
widespread and influential as they were in Marx's day.*

NICHOLAS LASH

*Religious man was born to be saved; psychological man was born to be
pleased.*

PHILIP RIEFF

*Sacrality and religiousness are alive and well as they always shall be, given
the human propensity for finding the numinous and hierophaneous in our
latest infatuations and for investing ultimacy in whatever serves our fancies.*

RICHARD WENTZ

To say that the contemporary discourse on medicine and religion is
anticipated by the work of Ludwig Feuerbach is not to say that it is
on a trajectory toward being a reductive account of religion that turns in
the end to no religion at all. For in spite of his being regularly counted
among the practitioners of the "hermeneutics of suspicion," Ludwig
Feuerbach clearly did not regard religion in purely negative terms.[1] He

sought rather to redescribe religion and in so doing to offer an account of religious belief that would free women and men from self-deception— from their unwarranted dependence on those gods whom he believed were nothing more than the anthropomorphic products of alienated human imaginations. His relative views of Christianity and other, more "primitive" religions seem to confirm this.

It is not clear, then, whether Feuerbach foresaw the abandonment of religion in general and god-talk in particular, or if he did, what sort of talk he proposed to replace it. According to D. Stephen Long, Feuerbach's interpretation of religion represents nothing other than the culmination of a modern "onto-theo-logic." According to one widely held view, this way of thinking theologically about the notion of being has its origins with the Nominalists of the late Middle Ages. In the discourse that has become ontotheology, "all speech of 'God' is a priori assumed to be based on a univocal understanding of our 'being' and God's 'being.'"[2] So Feuerbach, to the very real extent that he stands within this tradition, may well have been content to allow women and men to continue to believe in and worship something called "God," so long as they properly understood what they were doing. Which is to say, quite simply, that he wanted them to believe in and worship (i.e., to orient and live their lives toward) their best, idealized selves.

In his helpful book on Feuerbach, Van Harvey confirms this view. He suggests there that the account of religion that Feuerbach offered in his later work is not so hostile toward belief as is commonly thought. "Feuerbach, in principle, seems to classify religious beliefs as metaphysical even though they also suspiciously coincide with he deepest desires and wishes of humankind. But as Freud himself acknowledged, it does not follow because theism is an object of human wishes that it is thereby false. An illusion is not necessarily a delusion."[3] Feuerbach's interpretation of religion, says Harvey, is quite consistent with the liberal Protestant and (to a lesser extent) modern Catholic thought that has characterized a good deal of European and North American theology through the twentieth and into the twenty-first century. He compares Feuerbach to H. Richard Niebuhr (whose work he rightly understands to be representative of late twentieth-century liberal theology) and suggests that for both,

> The problem is whether one can attach faith, hope and love to this "slayer of all." It is whether one can have confidence in Being. A similar notion of faith may also be found in the writings of Protestant theologians such as Fritz Buri and Paul Tillich as well as in those of such Catholics as Karl Rahner and David Tracy. One might say they

all regard the problem of religious faith to be whether the great Void into which all things tumble, to use Alfred North Whitehead's phrase, can be seen as the great companion.[4]

According to Harvey, the great problem confronted by Feuerbach is the same one occupying the so-called ontotheologians. That is, they all wish to understand the manifold of "forces that impinge on the self." They all want to say something about whether, how, and to what extent those forces can or should be personified, worshiped, or perhaps even befriended and made useful.[5] What is most remarkable about Feuerbach's interpretation of religion is the extent to which it anticipates so much contemporary religion and discourse about religion. Contemporary religion and religiosity, often appearing in the guise of "spirituality," suggests that the manifold of forces impinging on the self can be not only personified but also domesticated, by our subjecting them, finally, to the logic of modern culture, which is essentially the logic of exchange and consumption. Thus contemporary religion regards the deity as an entity to be harnessed by individuals for their (self-defined) personal benefit. In what follows, we will show that to the same extent that the religion of the new rapprochement between religion and medicine conforms to the interpretation of religion embraced by the ontotheologians it is susceptible to a Christian theological critique of the culture of high modernity that sustains it.

|||
A Theological Critique—from a Curious Starting Place

We have suggested previously that the dominant religion of contemporary North America is radically individualized, radically self-interested, and radically therapeutic. As such, it offers little in the way of a critique of the sociopolitical status quo. Contemporary religion instead offers religious individuals a way of getting what they have come to believe they want and need, completely apart from their participation in particular common ways of life that may or may not challenge or offer an alternative to the existing order of things. Such a religion would seem to be susceptible to a critique analogous to the one leveled by one of Feuerbach's more critical appropriators, Karl Marx. Marx shared Feuerbach's critique of religion, in the sense that he saw religious belief as the alienating projection of certain human aspirations. Yet Marx went beyond Feuerbach in claiming that religion was also an ideological tool used by the wielders of power in modern, capitalist societies. "Feuerbach," Marx wrote, "resolves the religious essence into the *human* essence. But the human essence is no abstraction inherent in each single individual. In its reality it is the ensemble of social relations." Feuerbach, Marx believed, failed to "see that the 'religious sentiment' is itself a *social product*, and that the abstract individual whom he analyzes belongs in reality to a particular form of society."[6]

Marx argued that all consciousness, religious consciousness not excepted, "is therefore from the start a product of society, and it remains such as long as men exist at all."[7] In modern capitalist societies, Marx argued, the ruling classes used religion as one means of training the working classes to acquiesce to the existing sociopolitical order. Such formation, suggests Alasdair MacIntyre, has a twofold effect: religion "buttresses the established order by sanctifying it and by suggesting the political order is somehow ordained by divine authority, and it consoles the oppressed exploited by offering them in heaven what they are denied upon earth."[8]

Now, the point of our reference to Marx is not to claim that Marxist theory or the Marxist critique of religion is ultimately correct—as Christians, we are aware of some of the very significant theological limitations of Marxist theory.[9] Our point, rather, is to draw attention to two of Marx's more significant critical claims, which may or may not be related to one another: first, that every society, by virtue of the material conditions under which its members live with one another, produces in its inhabitants a particular consciousness. Second, insofar as "religion" is an inherent aspect of such societies, certain forms of false, alienating religious belief are inextricable aspects of all cultures formed by capitalist political economies.

These claims, the second in particular, are fundamentally theological. For the religion of which Marx was so critical was that highly subjective form of cultural, bourgeois Christianity descended via philosophical idealism from Kant, Schleiermacher, and Feuerbach.[10] Such a religion, which Marx believed was an opiate of the masses of workers in the industrial capitalist societies of his day, has a somewhat different role in the consumer-oriented capitalism of late modernity, a culture that Marx, optimistic as he was about the future demise of capitalism, could barely have anticipated.[11] Religion continues to serve the existing social order, not so much by pacifying the masses into accepting their fate in this life in expectation of a better life to come as by encouraging their participation in the logic of the market, and especially in the ethos of commodification. Religion and spirituality are transformed by the market into means, among others, of achieving a better life now.[12]

Karl Barth, the great Protestant critic of modern "religion," offers a perspective similar to that of Marx in observing that subjective religion is ever liable to being formed by the culture in which it exists:

> The religion of man is always conditioned absolutely by the way in which the starry heaven above and the moral law within have spoken to the individual. It is, therefore, conditioned by nature and climate, by blood and soil, by the economic, cultural, political, in short, the historical circumstances in which he lives. It will be an element in the habit or custom with which, quite apart from the question of truth and certainty, or rather at the very lowest and most rudimentary stages of his inquiry into it, he compounds with the terms of existence imposed upon him. But the terms of existence, and therefore custom, are variable.[13]

Barth saw, in other words, that a widely embraced religion originating within the self is always tempted to be self-serving, to help preserve and underwrite the order of things in whatever culture it occupies.[14] And in late modern culture, with its emphasis on the sovereignty of the individual, religion cannot help but be radically individualized. Robert Jenson notes:

> In the trend of modernity, our identifications of the good are eventually sanctioned only by the interests of groups. But so soon, of course, as this perception is itself reflexively noticed, no statement that something is good can be made in good faith, since the very purpose of such a statement is to restrain interest. Moreover, every community of interest is subject to endless further division by interest.[15]

Marx, Barth, and Jenson collectively make a point: the modern phenomena we call "religion," and "spirituality," which are always and everywhere the product of human subjectivity, attach themselves to, are shaped by, and sustain the cultures within which they operate, in no small part because human subjectivity in general is shaped by and sustains the culture within which it operates. This was true in the Berlin of Schleiermacher, it was true in the England of Marx and Engels, and it is true in North America at the beginning of the twenty-first century. In what follows, we want to show some of the ways that human subjectivity—and so religion and spirituality—are shaped in our own culture by the three characteristics of high modernity we have mentioned previously: radical individualism, narcissism, and the therapeutic quest.

III
The Culture of Late Modernity: Individualism

Volumes have been written about modernity and the way it schools its inhabitants to understand themselves as sovereign individuals whose chief end is the pursuit and cultivation of their own individual happiness. Alasdair MacIntyre, who must be counted among modernity's most rigorous critics, has argued that one of the effects of the so-called Enlightenment project that spawned modernity is the emergence of a particular understanding of the self. The self of modernity, he says, is formed to be "detached from all social particularity" and consequently is "set entirely over against the social world."[16] "The self thus conceived," he goes on to remark, "utterly distinct on the one hand from its social embodiments and lacking on the other any rational history of its own, may seem to have a certain abstract and ghostly character."[17]

It is thus at first glance something of a paradox that these claims of MacIntyre's about the social isolation of the modern individual subject come in the middle of a chapter that opens with the assertion that "a moral philosophy . . . characteristically presupposes a sociology."[18] But upon closer inspection this is not so much a paradox as simply a way of getting at the same point we are trying to make here, namely, that the asocial, ahistorical self of modernity is in large part the *product of* a modern society that forms its inhabitants to think of themselves as asocial and beyond the influence of historical contingency. And the most significant way in which modern society shapes the modern self is as an individual, "freed from hierarchy and teleology" and "sovereign in his moral authority."[19] The motto of modern individualism may be put thus: "I am what I myself choose to be."[20]

But if this disposition toward radical individualism is to some extent the product of modern society, we ought to be able to say something about the specific ways that modern society forms its inhabitants to be individuals. Moreover, in order to relate that formation to the specific concerns of our argument, we need to show something of its practical effects on modern agency, belief, and practice. According to the sociologist Anthony Giddens, the particular shape of modern *institutions* helps effect modern subjectivity.

Modernity, according to Giddens, is the name given to that postfeudal era in which societies are constituted by two institutional axes. The first of these is industrialism, "the social relations implied in the widespread use of material power and machinery in production processes." The second axis is capitalism, "where the term means a system of commodity production involving both competitive market products and the commodification of labor power." In addition, he says, modern institutions depend heavily on surveillance, which is the "supervisory control of subject populations" and which takes several forms, ranging from the (frequently internalized) supervisory observation of groups and individuals to the "use of information to coordinate social activities."[21]

And in societies so organized, certain kinds of bureaucratic and corporate institutions serve as substitutes for traditional community and its practices.[22] A level of human asociality is presumed by the existence of these institutions. They proceed from the assumption, derived in part from the uncritical acceptance of the Darwinian myth, which is itself one of the cornerstones of modernity, that we are at the deepest levels self-interested and therefore alienated from and at odds with one another.[23] Modern institutions thus purport to offer us ways to survive one another's proximity, while at the same time encouraging our further isolation by persuading us that there are unacceptable levels of risk inherent in our attempting to relate to one another beyond the structures of these institutions.[24]

And for persons so isolated from one another, reflexivity, a particular kind of self-surveillance, becomes a prominent feature of everyday life. "The reflexivity of modernity," says Giddens, "extends into the core of the self. Put in another way, in the context of a post-traditional order, the self becomes a *reflexive project*."[25] Because modernity has called into question and in some cases destroyed the integrity of those traditional social structures that once formed and informed personal identity, individuals become increasingly responsible not simply for the establishment and development but also for the ongoing recreation of their own identities.[26] "What the individual becomes is dependent on the continual reconstructive efforts in which she or he engages. These are far more than just 'getting to know oneself' better: self-understanding is subordinated to the more inclusive and fundamental aim of building/rebuilding a coherent and rewarding sense of identity."[27]

This project requires, notes Giddens, "continuous self-observation."[28] Moreover, the "line of development of the self is *internally referential*:

> The only significant connecting thread is the life trajectory as such. Personal integrity, as the achievement of an authentic self, comes from integrating life experiences within the narrative of self-development: the creation of a personal belief system by means of which the individual acknowledges that "his first loyalty is to himself." The key reference points are set "from the inside," in terms of how the individual constructs/reconstructs his life history.[29]

III
The Culture of Late Modernity: Narcissism

But all this self-talk, this emphasis on self-determination and self-actu-
alization, is, in the absence of traditional social structures and practices,
terribly problematic, leading to an emphasis on the welfare of the individual that borders on the pathological. For "as the spheres of public activity shrink, and cities become composed of thoroughfares rather than
open meeting places, the self is called upon to assume tasks with which it
cannot successfully cope."[30] The individual becomes the center of her
own private universe, a condition called narcissism.

> As a character disorder, narcissism is a preoccupation with the self
> which prevents the individual from establishing valid boundaries be-
> tween self and external worlds. Narcissism relates outside events to
> the needs and desires of the self, asking only "what this means to
> me." Narcissism presumes a constant search for self-identity, but this
> is a search which remains frustrated, because the restless pursuit of
> "who I am" is an expression of narcissistic absorption rather than a
> realisable [*sic*] quest. Narcissism stands in opposition to the commit-
> ment required to sustain intimate relationships; commitment places
> restrictions on the opportunities the individual has to sample the
> many experiences demanded in the search for self-fulfillment.[31]

The social critic Christopher Lasch argues that this inordinate attention to the actualization of the self has created a "culture of narcissism."
That culture shapes its members (if indeed the modern self can be
thought of as a "member" of anything) to be so fundamentally absorbed
with themselves that they are in every way walled off from each other.
Individuals are strangers and so potentially adversaries, not simply to
their contemporaries but also to those who have lived before them and
those who will follow them. In 1979, Lasch argued a point that is even
more the case in our own time:

> To live for the moment is the prevailing passion—to live for yourself,
> not for your predecessors or posterity. We are fast losing the sense of
> historical continuity, the sense of belonging to a succession of gen-
> erations originating in the past and stretching into the future. It is the
> waning of the sense of historical time – in particular, the erosion of
> any strong concern for posterity—that distinguishes the spiritual
> crisis of the seventies from earlier outbreaks of millenarian religion,
> to which it bears a superficial resemblance.[32]

The culture of narcissism thus advances a peculiar version of the modern understanding of history, and especially of history's meaning. According to the modern understanding, time marches impersonally and irresistibly forward, oblivious to and unconcerned with the well-being of humanity. Only the successful execution of what Gerald McKenny has called the Baconian project, which has as its goal to master history and "relieve the human condition of subjection to the whims of fortune or the bonds of natural necessity," offers solace to a beleaguered humanity.[33] The individual living in the culture of narcissism adopts an analogous view. Deprived of the institutions and practices that in traditional societies narrated the world and its history teleologically, institutions and practices that in traditional cultures gave meaning and helped cultivate identity and agency, the modern subject is presented with a set of decidedly stark alternatives: Either she can engage as an individual in a deliberate and sometimes obsessive cultivation of the self, or she can face the ostensive meaninglessness of life in a world whose history is potentially just "one damn thing after another." In such a world, what happens external to the self is largely beyond the control of the individual. It is the responsibility, finally, of each person to make use of whatever resources she can muster to live as authentically as possible, to achieve the greatest level of self-development. Friendship and neighborhood, parenting and marriage are all relatively unimportant, except as they can be used as means to the end of self-fulfillment.[34]

Moreover, the modern obsession with the technological mastery of contingency contributes to the expansion of narcissism. Modern culture does not offer its denizens a common good but an ever-increasing number of means of achieving whatever goods each individual chooses for himself or herself. Put more starkly, the self and its cultivation becomes each individual's private good.[35] As such, sickness, aging, and death, all threats to the isolated self of modernity, become new kinds of enemies against which the considerable weapons of modern science and technology are aimed. The so-called medicalization of aging questionably extrapolates from the steady increases in life expectancy since the beginnings of the scientific age and "assumes that medicine has the power to lengthen life still further and to abolish the horrors of old age."[36] And this new twist on the ancient, nearly universal human dread of death is not simply a product of late modernity but a force that strengthens its grasp.[37]

The denial of age in America culminates in the prolongevity movement, which hopes to abolish old age altogether. But the dread of age originates not in a "cult of youth" but in a cult of the self. Not only in its narcissistic indifference to future generations but in its grandiose vision of a technological utopia without old age, the pro-longevity movement exemplifies the fantasy of "absolute, sadistic power" which, according to Kohut, so deeply covers the narcissistic outlook. Pathological in its psychological origins and inspiration, su-perstitious in its faith in medical deliverance, the prolongevity move-ment expresses in characteristic form the anxieties of a culture that believes it has no future.[38]

|||

The Culture of Late Modernity: Therapeutics

We return, then, to that extreme reflexivity, that continual surveillance of the self, that is characteristic of modernity. In a culture where every per-son is trained repeatedly to look inward, to assess his or her feelings, and to ask how those feelings might be changed for the better, we should not be surprised to discover a pervasive therapeutic sensibility, where the ma-jority of persons live as if "nothing is at stake beyond a manipulable sense of well-being."[39] Indeed, as James Nolan notes, late modernity is by its very nature a therapeutic culture. The therapeutic perspective, he explains, "has become a taken-for-granted part of everyday life. It pro-vides culture with a set of symbols and codes that determine the bound-aries of moral life."[40]

The therapeutic culture has displayed a decidedly ambivalent attitude toward religion. On the one hand, therapy appears to have become a re-placement for religion. Nolan, among others, suggests that one of the characteristics of late modernity is the emergence of a "new priestly class" comprised of "psychologists, psychiatrists, counselors, therapists, and social workers," persons to whom the culture looks for authoritative answers about how to live a "good" life.[41]

Philip Rieff suggests that the key theorist in the early days of the therapeutic movement was Freud, who has been widely acknowledged as one of the most significant modern critics of religion. Freud was remarkable above all for his refusal as a therapist even to entertain the re-ligious question, the question of how we are "to be consoled for the misery of living."[42]

"Freud's was a severe and chill anti-doctrine, in which the awesome dichotomy with which culture imposes itself upon men—that between an ultimately meaningful and a meaningless life—must also be abandoned. This then was Freud's prescription to mankind as the patient, so that by the power of the analytic attitude a limit be set on the sway of culture over mankind."[43]

Freud's "gospel," says Rieff, was a gospel of "freer impulse" that saw humans "forever mediating between culture and instinct in an effort to gain some room for maneuver between these hostile powers. Maturity, according to Freud, lay in the trained capacity to keep the negotiations from breaking down."[44]

But such a purely analytic attitude, argues Rieff, threatened modern culture with a profound "symbolic impoverishment."[45] As such, it was inevitable that therapy itself would become more religious, in the sense that it would entertain increasingly individualized, increasingly narcissistic, versions of the religious question. It may be the case that "modern therapists must use the language of faith," but that language tends now to be profoundly self-referential.[46] It is oriented, in other words, almost totally to the satisfaction of need and desire without increasingly less attention to the propriety of desires or the ordering of needs. It is a "cultural revolution fought to no other purpose than greater amplitude and richness of living itself."[47]

The therapeutic attitude has thoroughly infected most (formerly) traditional North American religious communities. In spite of what the popular media tell us about how religion and spirituality are prospering, contemporary North American faith has become decidedly self-referential and obviously shaped by the therapeutic ethos. As Gary Dorrien explains in his helpful book *Soul in Society,* the relationship of Christianity in America to the lives of its adherents has over the course of the last 100 years or so come to be conducted in an increasingly therapeutic idiom. The language in many churches has become the language of needs; as one of our friends says, "tell us what yours are and let us supply them." And although it began there, this trend is no longer merely the purview of liberal Protestant Christianity.

> American fundamentalism no longer challenges the ethos of commercial society, as William Jennings Bryan did, but seeks to make individuals "whole" within it. Having set upon the goal of becoming successful and respectable in American society, fundamentalist preachers increasingly turn the gospel into a therapeutic balm for the anxieties of overstressed souls, finding impressive markets for their ministrations.[48]

|||

High Capitalism: The Material Condition of Possibility for the Triumph of the Therapeutic

Dorrien's references to "anxious consumers" of and "impressive markets" for therapeutic religion are scarcely accidental. The "triumph of the therapeutic" in contemporary North American religion and its role in the evolution of the new faith and health movement is simply one aspect, or perhaps one of the sequelae, of a more significant and profound set of social developments in late modernity. As Giddens and Lasch both point out, the therapeutic could not have triumphed except as part of an advanced capitalist political economy. An advanced form of capitalism, in other words, forms the basic material conditions of possibility for the existence of a pervasively therapeutic culture and radically therapeutic cultural religion.

High capitalism does not simply distribute goods and services; it also trains people to consume them uncritically and continually.[49] One of the watchwords of political economy in late modernity has been "economic growth": an economy that is not growing is "stagnant." This of course requires an expansion not simply of production but also of consumption. Christopher Lasch is not belaboring the obvious but making an often-overlooked point when he says that the "mass production of commodities in ever-increasing abundance demands a mass market to absorb them."[50]

The economy can expand only when there is perpetual dissatisfaction with the status quo; the potential consumer always must be convinced or in the process of being convinced that something important, even necessary, is absent from his or her life. Thus

> consumer capitalism . . . plays a basic role in furthering narcissism. . . . Consumption addresses the alienated qualities of modern social life and claims to be their solution: it promises the very things the narcissist desires . . . through the consumption of the "right" kind of goods and services. Hence all of us, in modern social conditions, live as though surrounded by mirrors; in these we search for the appearance of an unblemished, socially valued self.[51] And this search is the consequence of the work of one of the elements marking the transition to "high" or "late" capitalism: a particular kind of advertising.

> In a simpler time, advertising merely called attention to the product and extolled its advantages. Now it manufactures a product of its

own: the consumer, perpetually unsatisfied, restless, anxious, and bored. Advertising serves not so much to advertise products as to promote consumption as a way of life. It "educates" the masses into an unappeasable appetite not only for goods, but for new experiences and personal fulfillment.[52]

But the connections between late capitalism and the therapeutic culture—and the relevance of those connections to our project—are even more profound than we have indicated to this point. Consumerism is not *simply* an advanced or late stage of capitalism characterized by the infinite expansion of desire—what Crook, Pakulski, and Waters call "an 'endless wanting' on the part of consumers, who will 'not so much seek satisfaction from products, as pleasure from self-illusory experiences which they construct from their associated meanings.'"[53] Consumerism is also a logic. It is very nearly an entire way of life, a set of social practices and a form of social relationships through which traditional ways of life are challenged in the name of freedom or efficiency. In consumer capitalism people are fundamentally isolated from one another, except by the language and logic of exchange; even God is reduced to being simply another participant in the market and its mechanisms of exchange.[54]

These phenomena are part of the process of *commodification*, which is first of all a strictly economic (and here we use the word "economic" in the attenuated, simplistic sense of being strictly about the exchange of material goods and services) phenomenon through which it becomes possible to say (to coin a phrase) "everything has its price." Commodification entails the creation of the exchange value of a thing separate from its use value; the production and distribution of goods and services are abstracted from the particular persons or communities who produce and distribute them. This separation, however, does not remain strictly in the realm of the exchange of goods and services. It is a social phenomenon, as well, because it allows for "the disembedding of economic relations across indeterminate spans of time-space."[55] Put simply, desirable goods and services are bought and consumed with increasingly less contact with, interest in, or regard for the particular persons or communities who produced them.

In a culture dominated by the logic of commodification, it becomes nearly impossible, as we have heard Wendell Berry say, to give a "social history" of the things we possess and use. Not only do we not know who built our house or made our automobile or grew our food (or anything else we consume) or at what personal cost; we could for the most part care less, so long as we are pleased with the way these items satisfy our desire for them. That satisfaction may be based on their cost, performance, or appearance but is rarely based on their having been produced in a particular way or by particular persons or communities to whom we feel morally bound.

This is first of all a function of the efficiency inherent in capitalist modes of production and consumption. The social alienation effected by the brute mechanics of capitalism is well documented. Capitalism, through its commodification of labor, not only removes work from the household and divides the worker from the ultimate products of her work but also pulls her away from particular people and places in the name of more efficient production. The market regards such attachments as hindrances to the expansion of the economy.[56] The market, just because it is efficient, is radically impersonal. "There is no room," says Nicholas Boyle, "for any social units larger than the individual, and the individual has his identity only as a unit of consumption or of labor."[57] Identity is accounted for completely according to the logic of exchange, such that people are only interesting to the economy insofar as they produce or consume, and these without predetermined limits:

> They must not be tied to place, but prepared to move to follow employment. They must not be tied by time, but prepared to work all hours and days of the week, especially Sundays. It follows that they must not be tied to any particular group of people or community: that they have families, even, is of no social significance since it is of no significance in the market, except as distracting from their flexibility. . . . For only in this way can they meet the increasing and changing variety of the desires of the consumers. But who are the consumers? None other than the workers themselves. The assumption behind the demand for flexibility in the workers—which denies them the continuity of a fixed identity—is that as consumers too they will have no fixed or limited desires, not give themselves as identity by voluntarily renouncing any of those desires . . . for some more general—and therefore non-marketable—good.[58]

But consumerism is more than just the creation of a particular, highly efficient mechanics of production and consumption. It is not simply that economic life in consumer culture is separated from and so renders difficult the attachments and communal practices constituting traditional ways of life; it is also that consumer capitalism reforms subjectivity such that it is fundamentally destructive of the individual's *desire* for community and the concrete, storied social relationships that constitute community. In the capitalism of late modernity, Giddens points out, "individualism becomes extended to the sphere of consumption, the designation of individual wants becoming basic to the continuity of the system."[59] Yet this is largely hidden from view, insofar as it is a significant part of the "commodity structure" to present itself as scientific and objective. The basis of that structure, explains the late Marxist critic Georg Lukacs, "is that a relation between people takes on the character of a thing and thus acquires a 'phantom objectivity,' an autonomy that seems so strictly rational and all-embracing as to conceal every trace of its fundamental nature: the relation between people."[60]

And this is not simply a matter of the foundational capitalist-Darwinian assertion of the inherent self-interestedness of every woman and man, which, in its own way, as it is accepted as unquestionable truth, actually serves to *make* women and men self-interested.[61] It is also a matter of the peculiar way that our own latest stage of capitalism brings about this transformation of subjectivity. Exchange, understood in strictly capitalist economic terms, attains what John Milbank calls a kind of "ontological primacy" that tends to reduce every human interaction to the logic of exchange.[62] And when women and men come to think of other women and men (among other things) primarily according to the logic of exchange—that is, either as strangers and potential adversaries or as contractual suppliers of goods and services—community becomes an impossibility. For:

> Capitalism of its most innate tendency precludes community. This is because (let us remind ourselves), it makes the prime purpose of society as a whole and also of individuals to be one of accumulation of abstract wealth, or of power-to-do-things in general, and rigorously subordinates any desire to do anything concrete in particular, including the formation of social relationships. Where individuals are commanded "accumulate!" it will not be possible to restrict their accumulation except through the rules of a regulated struggle of all with all. And where society recognizes only the general imperative "accumulate!" it will not be possible to arrive at any notion of an intrinsically just distribution of roles, resources and rewards. Instead, a set of rules for exchanges between *things* which reduces them all to a fictional abstract measure, will both disguise and organize (as Marx realized) relationships of arbitrarily unequal power.[63]

It is precisely here that the forces of late capitalism most significantly reconfigure human subjectivity. Everything (and everybody) becomes an object to the capitalist subject, and so everything (and everybody) is susceptible to being regarded strictly according to the logic of exchange.[64]

That logic insists (incorrectly) that the "market is in human nature" and that everything is best understood according to the logic of the market.[65] Thus in late capitalism (as we have already suggested), consumption and production are in many and several ways conflated, such that consumer desire uncritically legitimates itself and "consumption is explicitly described as the production of a commodity or a specific utility; in other words, a use value which can be anything from sexual gratification to a convenient place to take it out on your children if the outside world becomes inclement."[66]

In consumer culture, nothing is finally more real than the commodity form. Lukacs calls this phenomenon reification, and he says it "requires that a society should learn to satisfy all it needs in terms of commodity exchange."[67] This includes the need not simply for membership in a concrete human community but also for participation in ways of life that might finally make life worth living. This is deeply ironic: the same culture that produces an extraordinary homogenization of consciousness also tacitly schools women and men to pursue the deepest forms of satisfaction—as individuals, according to the logic of exchange. Thus "the relations between men that lie hidden in the immediate commodity relation, as well as the relations between men and the objects that should really gratify their needs, have faded to the point where they can be neither recognized nor even perceived."[68]

| | |

Health and Happiness as Commodities: Medicine and Religion as Media and Methods of Exchange

Insofar as the traits that we have suggested are characteristic of modern subjectivity—the individualism, the narcissism, and the therapeutic ethos—are produced by the latest stage of capitalism, the contemporary rapprochement between medicine and religion, especially in its more popular manifestations, is in part due to the unprecedented and unrestricted expansion of the commodity form. Divided from one another by suspicion and by desire for the same ostensibly scarce goods, loosened from ways of life that might once have formed us to live and to die well together, we are left alone, not so much to find meaning but to pursue the satisfaction—of precisely those desires created by widespread commodification. We are formed by the market apparatus to be consumers, and the same apparatus offers us the technical means to acquire the things we need and the things we have been taught to want. And religion is not excepted from this way of thinking. Indeed, religion is at its very center.

In chapter 1, we entertained the possibility that contemporary medicine's current fascination with religion was simply the reestablishment of an ancient concord. That is, we suggested it might be a repristination, or restoration, of the ethos characteristic of an age when health and healing were understood to encompass not simply the discovery and destruction of disease but the mending of relationships with community, earth, and deity, as well. As it turns out, however, the contemporary rapprochement is something else entirely. It resembles the old way only in that it presumes a now-perverse, exchange-oriented interconnection between a therapeutic deity, an ultimately self-interested and acquisitive spirituality, and a radically individualized, utilitarian account of health. Such an account of health can be called "holistic," but only in the sense that its definition derives from multiple sources, as much from the market and the logic of exchange as from its being specified by medical science.

A theologically adequate account of health is the first victim of this new, distinctly modern, holism. What it means to "be healthy" is subtly transformed, and in that transformation health is broken loose from its moorings to the daily life of particular communities of people living in particular places at particular times and united by particular practices. The advocates of the new rapprochement would probably concur with Karl Barth's definition of health as not simply the absence of disease but also the "capability, vigor and freedom . . . the strength for human life . . . the integration of the psycho-physical functions," which he summarizes as "the strength to be as man."[69] Yet they would also find it difficult to make sense—at least as an integral part of their conceptualization of the relation of health with religious belief and practice—of his further admonition that:

> The principle *mens sana in corpore sano* can be a highly short-sighted and brutal one if it is only understood individually and not in the wider sense of *in societate sana*. And this extension cannot only mean that we must see to it that the benefits of hygiene, sport and medicine are made available for all, or at least as many as possible. It must mean that the general living conditions of all, or at least of as many as possible, are to be shaped in such a way that they make not just a negative but a positive preventative contribution to their health, as is the case already in varying degrees with the privileged. The will for health of the individual must therefore take also the form of the will to improve, raise and perhaps radically transform the general living conditions of all men.[70]

In the radically individualized consumer culture of late modernity, health as "the strength to be as man" may no longer be understood primarily, as Wendell Berry says it must, in terms of a person's being properly united by the grace of the Creator to her " place and all its creatures."[71] Rather, the strength to be becomes the strength to will one's participation in the world. But in modernity, the world is the market. The market has become the locus of the pursuit of satisfaction and meaning; it is the place one turns to make exchanges for the things one wants, as well as the way one thinks about acquiring those things.

Health, however, is not only the capacity to participate in the modern practices of exchange, acquisition, and consumption. It is also a commodity among others to be pursued and acquired *through* those practices, now expanded to include religious practices. So understood, health is a good example of what Marx would have called a *fetishized* commodity; it is pursued and acquired based on its use value, according to the logic of exchange, and without respect to the persons, practices, or resources responsible for its production.[72]

This is not to say that God is absent from this particular logic of exchange. It is rather to say that God is transformed and defined by that logic. God is no longer one who definitively shows up in human history, giving godself and making godself known in particular ways to particular people. God is no longer one whose particular saving acts reveal God's nature and relationship to the creation. God is no longer one whose definitive acts suggest the proper shape and texture and working of the creation.[73] (Such a God would be, in the language of one of the new rapprochement's popularizers and strongest advocates, terribly "overdetermined.")[74] Rather, the God of the contemporary rapprochement is essentially reduced to the reification of desire. As such, God comes to be a placeholder in the logic of exchange: the abstract, faceless producer of, among other things, that exchangeable, acquirable commodity called health. Its peculiarly late-modern nature notwithstanding, this is a God Feuerbach would easily have recognized; it is a projection of a somewhat more medicalized version of the rage-to-live.

|||

The Domesticated God of the Exchange

The God of the contemporary rapprochement is thus a domesticated God. God is domesticated in the sense that the places and modes of God's activity are restricted, not by God but by those who refer to God. "Domestication refers to the manner in which something is tamed, transformed to comply with our pragmatic need for amenity and utility. It is to create a *domus*, a domicile in which everything must fit or conform; to define things, people, and animals by the décor, confinement, and feigned permanence of our *domus*."[75] A domesticated God is never anything more or less than those who believe in that God they wish God to be. This, then, is another way to understand the story of modernity and its ontotheology: it is the story of the construction of a market-shaped domus for God.

This is a story we have already told, but it is worth reiterating in slightly different form. We have already spoken, following Nicholas Lash, John Milbank, and D. Steven Long, of the trend, during the period in which the Middle Ages gave way to modernity, toward an increasingly univocal use of language.[76] The point at which that tendency enables the domestication of God is in the emergent modern understanding of "being." Whereas Thomas Aquinas had argued that "God's relation to being is just totally different from anything else's relation to being, and we cannot imagine what "being" means as applied to God," some of those who came after him thought otherwise.

> Created things, they said, are something and not nothing, and so is God, and so they share the property of "being." Scotus even said that one can attribute "being" univocally to both God and creatures. . . . Both God and creatures have being and therefore, understanding what "being" means in reference to creatures, we can extend the usage to God by analogy of internal attribution. Creatures are, and God causes them to be. So, just as we can say that the fire must be at least as hot as the pan, so we can say that God must have at least as much being—and in the same sense of "being"—as the things God creates.[77]

Whether or not the nominalists are to blame, it is clearly the case that one of the characteristics of modernity is the emergence of the univocal use of the notion "being," which enables the objectification of God. Once God and creatures are thought to "be" in roughly the same manner, a new way of differentiating God from creatures becomes necessary. "God is faced with classifications of objectivity. God becomes transcendent, the question of possible immanence becoming problematical."[78]

> God was now "up there" or "out there," looking *at* us and we *at* God. God was no longer a mysterious inexhaustible presence, *like* the wind or the sound of words. As a matter of fact, now that God was objectified, it was possible to wonder whether such an objective, absolute,

singular can really *be*. If God exists, it may be at a great distance, so great we may wonder what to do with God. Shall we hang on to the notion of God's objective reality as a kind of last resort? Having objectified this reality, we discover that we are in a position to *do* something with it, to it, or even to ignore it in its remoteness.[79]

And so we see from a slightly different perspective the distinctly modern problem of locating and describing God, but this time with a twist; it now becomes possible and even advisable, on theological terms, to render God useful. Duns Scotus argued that in both God and humans, "the will is primary to the intellect," meaning, in effect, that the most important thing about God (and us) is our free, autonomous capacity to will.[80] And where God is regarded as radically transcendent, there is a tendency toward the conflation of the human will with the divine. If humans, like God, are *"ens singularissimam*—objective individuals," then relations between humans and God will tend always to assume a quintessentially modern form: the contract.[81] Just so, in the late capitalism of our own day, the relation between humans and God finds its domicile in that variation on the contract that is the logic of exchange.

God is defined by the logic of exchange as a producer of desirable commodities to be exchanged as a matter of course for particular kinds of devotional behaviors, such as prayer, meditation, or church attendance. Now, understood within the contexts of the several religious traditions from and within which they typically are engaged—certainly this is the case for the Christian tradition—such religious behaviors are properly understood as practices. According to Alasdair MacIntyre, a practice is a

> coherent and complex form of socially established cooperative
> human activity through which goods inherent to that form of ac-
> tivity are realized in the course of trying to achieve those standards
> of excellence which are appropriate to, and partially definitive of, that
> form of activity, with the result that human powers to achieve excel-
> lence, and human conceptions of the goods involved, are systemati-
> cally extended.[82]

Within the logic of exchange, however, devotional behaviors are reduced, in effect, to techniques. Techniques are forms of action that are expected to produce specific, objective results that are external and instrumental to the actions themselves, without respect to their embeddedness in particular ways of life.[83] Practices may also produce goods external to the action, but that is not their primary point. The ends at which practices aim explicitly are always internal to the ways of life in which they are embedded; this cannot be said of techniques, because technique does not require being embedded in a way of life. To put the distinction perhaps a bit too sharply, the primary point of practices is the activities themselves and the kind of person they form, while the primary point of techniques is the immediate results they produce *for* the person employing them. Techniques are effective in the sense that they can produce results; various types of devotional activity, engaged in simply for the purpose of achieving some immediate, external end, like physical well-being, may be effective for the achievement of that end. But such activities are no longer practices, because they have been divorced from their proper social context.

Just to the extent that practices such as prayer, meditation, Scripture reading, and service have been transformed and reduced to techniques, that transformation has contributed to the modern domestication of God. Divorced from the context of a particular traditional story of particular redemptive acts, God is simply that ultimate objective Other to whom devotional activity is directed. In the late modern context, God is not so much the one who wills the health of God's creatures as a sign of God's care for the creation, as the one whose will is bound instrumentally by and to the logic of exchange. For if the human relation to God is essentially contractual—that is, if it is technical and instrumental—then God becomes obligated to fulfill the contract by providing health in exchange for devotion. And this is a tragedy, for theologically, it matters very little whether the exchange actually "works" in terms of its effect on health; improvements to the health of persons of faith notwithstanding, something is lost when the interrelationship of faithfulness and healthfulness is reduced to exchange.[84]

What is lost, or at least threatened, is that form of social life peculiar to the Christian community, a form that emerges from and is based in the community's worship and imitation of the triune God. The community formed by that worship and that imitation is a community that has always understood the significance of hospitality, of welcoming into its midst and embracing that which is other—especially when the other is conspicuously dependent. The commitment to hospitality has been the basis of Christian attitudes toward the sick, inspiring the creations of hospitals—places of hospitality and care for the sick.[85]

But this form of life is threatened precisely because the Christian commitment to be hospitable and patiently present to the sick is a reflection of the God that Christians worship. The Christian God is himself patient and hospitable. Perhaps most important, the Christian God is a God who suffers in solidarity with the sufferings of the creation. In the Christian tradition, this is the primary form taken by God's love for the creation. This is not, however, the God of modernity, the God of the ontotheologians, or the God of the logic of exchange.

The difference between these two is significant. The theologian John Howard Yoder has said:

> The work of God is the calling of a people, whether in the Old Covenant or the new. The church is then not simply the bearer of the message of reconciliation, in the way a newspaper or telephone company can bear any message with which it is entrusted. Nor is the church simply the result of a message, as an alumni association is the product of a school or the crowd in the theater is the product of the reputation of the film. That men and women are called together to a new social wholeness is itself the work of God, which gives meaning to history, from which both personal conversion (whereby individuals are called into this meaning) and missionary instrumentalities are derived.[86]

This means, among other things, that God's redemptive work *is* a witness-bearing community whose common life reflects to the world the character of God's redemptive love. The world understands that God is patient and hospitable and long-suffering, in other words, because the people of God are patient and hospitable and long-suffering. And the people of God can be patient, hospitable, and long-suffering only because and just to the extent that the God whom they worship is patient, hospitable, and long-suffering.

But what if that people begins to worship another God, one whose concern for the world is domesticated by the logic of exchange, one who is reduced, however unintentionally, to being one who gives individuals health in exchange for their devotion? Their self-understanding and their common life, because they are derived from the God they worship, will also change. For once health is made, however implicitly, a *product* of individual devotional activity, devotion will necessarily be directed toward the achievement of health. And when devotion is directed toward the achievement of health, the community's attitude toward the sick and the suffering, toward those who cannot, no matter what they do, become healthy, will inevitably be changed.

The work of God in the world is the calling and the formation of a people. But that work requires of that people their worship of the God to whom they strive to bear witness. The Christian God is not a God who can be domiciled in the logic of exchange; such a God is an idol, at best an attenuation of the God Christians worship. The difference and the significance of that difference requires a proper account of God's saving acts and of the way of life engendered by the worship of that God, a task to which we turn in the following chapters.

The Faithfulness of the Cross and the Idol of the Therapeutic

*By the beginning of the twenty-first century, we may observe the results of
. . . domestication. Protestantism has become a form of modern religionism
that has been successful in transforming most of American religious life,
including that of Roman Catholics, Jews, and Buddhists, into its own image.
The rigorous intellectualism of rabbinic Jews and the classical theological
vision of Roman Catholic thinkers have been successfully manipulated by the
pragmatic assumptions of modern life, and the Dalai Lama sounds like
Norman Vincent Peale or Robert Schuller.*

RICHARD WENTZ

*God alone is truly independent. He alone belongs wholly to Himself and lives
in and by Himself. Man's creaturely existence as such is not his property; it is
a loan. As such it must be held in trust. It is not, therefore, under the control
of man. But in the broadest sense it is meant for the service of God. . . .
This is the simplest information that can be given regarding the fact and
meaning of life. Nor is it the result of self-reflection on the part of man. It
depends entirely on the fact that God addresses him. It derives from the Word
of God as the Word of his Creator and Lord. And implicitly it is the information which is given concerning all other life and the reality and meaning of
life in general.*

KARL BARTH

There is a great irony in the several varieties of the admonition,
so frequently extended by the champions of the contemporary
rapprochement, not to "overdetermine" God. For that very admonition
carries along, contains or at least presumes a notion of God that already
is, at least by the standards of historical Christianity, radically overdetermined. The deity of the contemporary rapprochement, who is generally

and for the most part equivalent to the generic cultural deity of contemporary North America, is determined not by the narrative histories of any of those ancient traditions we call "the religions" but by the instrumental, therapeutic reason of this latest stage of modernity. And such a deity, one who ostensibly is a creature of human belief, one domesticated within the logic of the market and offering health or happiness in exchange for—or what, in the final analysis, is reducible to exchange for—devotion, is far more "determined" than the divinity of the Christian tradition. The Christian God, in spite of popular imaginings, remains radically free and so always beyond domestication by creatures. Thus a God domesticated by any form of human agency is, from the perspective of the Christian tradition, an idol—and this in spite of the possible resemblances to the Christian God that such a deity might bear.

This means that the evocation of some generic "religion," or especially of a generic "spirituality" that is in any way dependent on human agency, ought at the very least to arouse among Christians certain theological suspicions. But even in the midst of those suspicions, we must acknowledge that the human yearning to transcend the everyday appears to be ubiquitous. What then should we make of the apparently transcultural pervasiveness of this yearning? In his widely read book *Timeless Healing*, Herbert Benson, reflecting, in part, on the apparent ubiquity of belief, says that his work at the intersection of spirituality and health has led him to conclude that we are "wired for God . . . custom-made to engage in and exercise beliefs."[1] Religion and spirituality, in other words, are "natural" phenomena that exist on the most fundamental biological level:

> Whether or not God exists, our genes guarantee that we will bear faith and that our bodies will be soothed by believing in some antithesis to mortality and human frailty. So that we will not be incapacitated by the acknowledgment and dread of death, our brains harbor beliefs in a better, nobler meaning to life.[2]

Therefore, just to the extent that all humans share the same biology—that is, to the extent that we all desire health and are faced with the prospect of sickness, suffering, and death—we also share basically the same (tendency toward) yearning for spiritual gratification. The two are inseparable. Benson's remarkable resemblance to Feuerbach—at least on this one point—notwithstanding, we must consider the possibility that he is at least partly right. Cursorily, women and men in every culture *do* seem to want to be healthy and happy. Moreover, a constellation of human activities, which have resembled each other enough to be given the common label "religious," *has* existed across the boundaries of time and culture. And because the contemporary rapprochement between religion and medicine is so fundamentally dependent on these apparent universalities, any Christian theological interrogation of the claims of that alliance must attend first of all to the dependence of those claims on the existence of something like a universal spirituality or religiosity.

For help at this point we may turn again to the work of Karl Barth, who was especially conscious of the peculiar relationship of historical Christianity to modern thinking about religion and spirituality.[3] In chapter 4 we quoted his warning about the potential dangers associated with some universal notion of "human spirituality" or generic "religion as such." Barth saw that this kind of religion is problematic because it is always susceptible to cooptation by the broader culture within which it exists. Precisely because such religion presumes to be independent of social or cultural particularity, it is in the end largely plastic and so is shaped blindly by the practices of whatever culture it happens to inhabit. It is thus "conditioned by nature and climate, by blood and soil, by the economic, cultural, political, in short, the historical circumstances in which [one] lives."[4] The very denial of the particularity of religious belief is what allows women and men to be captive to what is finally always a socially and culturally shaped aspect of human existence. And Barth saw this as dangerous because he understood so well the pervasive temptation toward idolatry facing the person or community who attempts to speak or act on behalf of God.[5]

This is not to suggest that there is no religion. Barth understood and asserted that there *is* a sense in which something like what is typically referred to as "religion" is (for want of a better word) "natural."[6] On the one hand, he says, that which takes place at the intersection of humanity and divinity is always, if and to the extent that it is *truthful*, the self-revealing work of God and God alone; "both the reality and the possibility of this event," he explains, "are the being and action only of God, and especially of God the Holy Spirit. Both the reality and the possibility!"[7] Yet, he concedes, because "this revelation is in fact an event which encounters man," it "has *at least the form* of human competence, experience and activity. . . . It has at least the aspect and character of a human phenomenon."[8] Were there not humans who were, to use Benson's phrase, in some sense "wired for God," there would *be* no religion. And the human aspect and character of the phenomenon suggests that:

We can inquire into its nature and structure and value as we can in the case of all others. We can compare it with other phenomena of a more or less similar type. We can understand it and judge it according to the comparison. But the sphere to which this problem introduces us is the sphere of religion.[9]

III

The Sphere of "Religion"

Among the things the Christian discovers upon entry into this problem—what Barth calls the "sphere of religion"—is that there is at least an apparent analogy between her own faith and those other traditions she has learned to call the religions, "there is," says Barth, "this general human element which we cannot avoid or call by any other name."[10] Religion, it seems, is just about everywhere.

> Always and even necessarily men seem to feel that they are confronted by definite forces which stand over their own life and that of the world and influence it. Even at the most primitive cultural levels they seem to be aware not only of human nature but also of the spirit and of spirits and their operation. Human culture in general and human existence in detail seem always and everywhere to be related by men to something ultimate and decisive, which is at least a powerful rival to their own will and power. Both culture and existence seem to have been determined or partly determined by a reverence for something ostensibly more than man, for some Other or wholly Other, for a supreme Relative or even the Absolute. There seems always and everywhere to be an awareness of the reality and possibility of a dedication, or even a sanctification of the life of man, on the basis of an individual or social striving, which is almost always and everywhere referred to an event which comes from beyond.[11]

So long as that which lies beyond human being remains a mystery, religion will exist. This is as close as Barth gets to Schleiermacher and his heirs. But the proximity is only apparent. For in spite, says Barth, of the fact that religion is always in some sense "a vital utterance and activity of . . . man," the Christian must keep always in mind the sense in which the self-revelation of God to the world in the stories of Israel, Jesus, and the Church also represents a subversion of the notion that there exists a universal human spirituality.[12] And this means that there will always be a sense in which religion and spirituality as such are idolatrous antitheses to God's particular self-revelation in history. Just to the extent that the Christian clings to any notion of religion apart from or prior to its being solely the effect of God's particular self-revelation in Israel, Jesus, and the church, she also clings to a notion of God that is potentially idolatrous.

Christianity can never be understood properly as one species among others of a generic "religion." This is not a denial of the possibility that God has revealed godself in or to other traditions; rather, it is an assertion that there is no broad, neutral platform above or beyond any *specific* religious tradition or any *particular* display of spirituality from which to adjudicate such matters. The religions and their deities cannot be conflated and can be compared only in a limited way. For the Christian, God has been and is *really present* to the world in Jesus of Nazareth and in the church, which is his body. As such, the relationship of that body to the religions cannot be specified in principle, especially by an appeal to some ostensibly neutral notions, like religion-as-such or spirituality-as-such.[13]

This assertion seems to raise the question of where the Christian might stand in order to adjudicate faithfully the various claims of the contemporary rapprochement. Given the assumptions and assertions of the modern culture of which the contemporary rapprochement is so clearly a part, it would appear that such judgments must be made solely on the basis of the movement's empirical-statistical claims to efficacy. To do that, however, will be to repeat the fundamental error that Michael Buckley says theologians made at the cusp of the Enlightenment: they attempted to articulate the Christian account of reality in the language of the emergent scientific and philosophical discourse.[14] In so doing, they disregarded a central Christian claim, that reality is to be encountered neither simply in the quantifiable realm of the empirical nor in the ephemeral realm of abstract and private human reflection but in the everyday, "quotidian" practices through which members of the Christian community reenact the stories of God's activity toward creation.[15] It is these practices that create the "real" world in which Christians live and by which they make ultimate sense of their lives in both sickness and health.

|||

Speaking of God

The difference is vital, for "no word . . . is more difficult to use appropriately than 'God.'"[16] It is for this reason, Nicholas Lash suggests, that the "primary function of Christian doctrine is regulative rather than descriptive. As regulative, its purpose is to protect correct reference: to help us set our hearts on God (and not something which we mistake for God) and make true mention of him."[17] It is easy to make untrue mention of God, not because we are not given to speech about matters of ultimate significance but because our understanding of such matters and our speech about them is so susceptible to distortion by the languages and practices of the culture(s) in which we live. And this is especially true of those views of and languages about God that identify God with that which is radically "beyond," in the realm of nondiscursive transcendence. A deity so identified is beyond human grasp—but only in a sense. For such a deity is one that can *only* be imagined and, as it turns out, *is* therefore only to be *imagined*. And the untrained human imagination, like all untrained human faculties, is, according to the Christian narrative, formed and informed—in part, at least—by our separation from God and so tends toward idolatry.

But the Christian God is not an idea, not the product of speculation about what lies "beyond" the realms of sensibility or thought.[18] And Christianity is not a variety of religion. Rather, it is a particular interpretation of a particular, densely material *history*—the history of those particular, densely material events through which the self-giving God of Israel, Jesus, and the church has worked and is working out the redemption of creation.[19] That history centers on a particular event, the incarnation, by which God's "Word became flesh." This is an utterance, says Nicholas Lash, which can also be put in the form of a particular historical statement: "the flesh became Word. Human history produced, from its own resources (which are, not *alternative* to divine resources—to the resources of grace—but their contingent, empirical form), the individual in whom the mystery of God and his promise is historically actualized, disclosed, shown, spoken."[20]

Materialism is not reductionism; "the 'materialist' assertion that 'the flesh became Word' does not contradict the assertion that 'the Word became flesh,' but gives it historical expression."[21] Similarly, belief (or faith) is itself historical and material—it is the ongoing reproduction of the particular history of God's saving activity among a gathered community of persons. Belief does presume something like the human capacity to believe, but it is always more than *just* that capacity. Belief is fundamentally that gift created by God's saving activity as it is displayed in and produced by those concrete practices by which the community reenacts and so performs its history.[22]

This suggests that the primary task of Christian theology (as a voice of and for the Christian community) is continually to retell the particular history that is giving rise to and being performed in those practices. "The task of such a theology, says John Milbank, "is not apologetic, nor even argument. Rather it is to tell again the Christian *mythos*, pronounce again the Christian *logos*, and call again for Christian *praxis* in a manner that restores their freshness and originality."[23] Such telling, proclaiming, and calling, if they are faithful, will not simply pose Christianity as a story or stories among others, which women and men might use to negotiate the world more successfully or with a greater sense of fulfillment. Rather, they will pose the stories of Christianity as actually *creating* the world in which teller and hearer live—the *same* world. "These stories are not situated within the world: instead, for the Christian, the world is situated within these stories. They define for us what reality is, and they function as 'metanarrative' . . . in the sense of a story privileged by faith, and seen as the key to the interpretation and regulation of all other stories."[24]

Among the more circumscribed "stories" situated within the stories of Israel, Jesus, and the church are those that gesture toward particular and proper accounts of sickness, suffering, healing, and caring. But these stories can be understood and articulated only as they are "stood under," and this requires that disciplined reordering of thought, speech, and desire called Christian discipleship. As Christians, we can think rightly about faith and health only as we are trained rightly to worship God—and this is not an easy matter. The problem is not that women and men have no taste for religion but that we are religious gluttons. Our religious inclinations are profoundly subject to distortions, which can be corrected only as we are immersed in the Christian story. Such immersion is, finally, only possible in that community that is created by the story and charged with its performance.[25] Discipleship is in large measure a matter of learning to perform the story in and with the church.

Insofar as Christian discipleship is the performance of the Christian story, it is a merger of story and practice. Insofar as discipleship is a matter of *divinization*, of what is sometimes in the Eastern Christian tradition called theosis, the story to be performed is the story of God's saving activity toward creation, in and through which God unites creatures to godself. Discipleship is therefore a participation in the church's performance of the canonical stories of the life, death, and resurrection of Jesus of Nazareth. What Christians know of God is always and everywhere determined by God's making godself known in the life and teachings of the man Jesus. It is a central claim of the Christian tradition that God speaks paradigmatically in and through Jesus' speech and action; this is a central meaning of the claim that Jesus is God's Word: "God's Word means that God speaks," and "in the vocabulary of Trinitarian doctrine God's Son cannot be differentiated from God's Word."[26] God's speech is therefore *personal*.[27]

God's speech, precisely because it is personal, is also particular. Barth says that the claim that Jesus of Nazareth is God's Word to and for creation is itself "the objective possibility of revelation." The God who cannot otherwise be rightly known "wills to veil Himself by becoming a man, in order by breaking out of the veiling to unveil himself as a man. He wills to be silent and yet to speak."[28] This is not a generic claim about human nature or the fundamental capacity of humanity to speak for God; "it has nothing to do with the attempt to prove a special property in man as such to be a bearer of the revelation of God."[29] Rather, it is a claim about one particular man, namely Jesus of Nazareth.

> Certainly in *Jesus Christ*, as he is attested in Holy Scripture, we are not dealing with man in the abstract: not with the man who is able with his modicum of religion and religious morality to be sufficient unto himself without God and thus to be God. But neither are we dealing with *God* in the abstract: not with one who in His deity exists only separated from man, distant and strange and thus a nonhuman if indeed not an inhuman God. In Jesus Christ there is no isolation of man from God or of God from man.[30]

This means that the reality we call Christianity and therefore the very possibility of true Christian faith is absolutely dependent on this one man. "The name of Jesus Christ alone has created the Christian religion. Without Him it would never have been."[31] And this is not merely a historical claim about the origins of one way among others of being religious or of manifesting an innate human spirituality. "For if we would speak of the Christian religion as a reality, we cannot be content merely to look back at its creation and historical existence. We have to think of it in the same way we think of our own existence and that of the world, as a reality which is to be and is created by Jesus Christ yesterday and today and tomorrow."[32]

The dependence of our own existence on the existence of Jesus is not merely one of true belief but of true flourishing. Through her immersion in the church's practiced reenactment of the stories of Jesus' life and teachings, the Christian discovers the true End of her life, which is friendship with God in Christ; it is by participating in that communal reality founded by and forever dependent on Jesus that she may reach that End.[33] Just so, in a very profound way the true good of every woman and man is first of all *given by* and *displayed* in the life of Jesus, the exemplary human. This good contains and includes all other goods. It is attainable in its fullness only eschatologically; yet eschatology is not, properly understood, purely a matter of waiting for something better or something different to be realized in a time yet to come. Our blessedness is defined by our participation in God in Christ, yet it is at the same time *our* blessedness, recognizable as such.[34] Things we genuinely want, things for which we genuinely long, constitute it.

> As the promise interprets the antecedent hopes and fears of some community, these in turn necessarily interpret the promise. To a community destroyed by violence, the prophet rightly promised the peace to be made by Messiah's rule, which will be both recognizable after the fact as the fulfillment of their longings and beyond anything they could otherwise have envisioned. For those able to think only of a next meal a vision of the Son's Wedding-Banquet is neither unspiritual nor "pie in the sky." To a Rome that still remembered its founding dream of republic but had forgotten its meaning Augustine proclaimed the coming Polity of God. Eschatological descriptions emerge as the other side of the same event of interpretation in which the gospels ethics emerge.[35]

|||

Living and Longing for Health

This interdependence of ethics with eschatology suggests also the interdependence of the question "For what shall we hope?" with the question "How then shall we live?" The hope is for the fulfillment of a promise, and the promise is not separable from the One who makes it. But the One who makes the Christian eschatological promise is also the One who specifies the path by which that promise may be reached. And so here we may attempt to frame the problematic that gives rise to the concerns of this book: "How are a people whose greatest Good is the worship of and friendship with a crucified God supposed to think about and live with respect to their own and others' sickness and suffering?"

Every faithful answer to the question of what might constitute a fulsome yet faithful Christian response to sickness and suffering must begin and end with reference to the cross and resurrection of Jesus of Nazareth. Insofar as Christianity makes possible, proclaims, and promises a victory *over* suffering, it makes possible, proclaims, and promises a victory *through* the suffering and resurrection of Jesus. His death and resurrection are for Christians *the* place of God's self-revelation and of God's saving work; the death of Christ is "*the* parable of the Kingdom."[36]

His entering within the deepest darkness of human ambiguity and abiding within it is THE faithfulness. The life of Jesus is perfected obedience to the will of the faithful God. Jesus stands among sinners as a sinner; He sets himself wholly under the judgment under which the world is set; He takes His place where God can be present only in questioning about Him; He takes the form of a slave; He moves to the cross and to death; His greatest achievement is a negative achievement.[37]

This is the significance of the incarnation: the Word, the second person of the triune God, became flesh, named Jesus, and he was made "perfect through sufferings . . . in every respect tested as we are, yet without sin."[38] As women and men suffer, so did Jesus suffer; as women and men die, so did Jesus die. Christianity calls for a peculiar and complex disposition toward the limits given to women and men by their often fragile and always mortal bodies. Rather than promise any immediate or unconditional deliverance from these conditions, the Christian tradition calls on its adherents to embrace them as possibilities. The New Testament language of discipleship is to a very significant extent a language that juxtaposes the life of the disciple to the life of her Lord. It exhorts to a kind of imitation of and participation in the life of Jesus, especially with respect to his service to others and his proclamation in word and deed of the coming reign of God's redemptive love. It suggests the likelihood of sharing in his suffering and goes so far as to encourage, at least in certain circumstances, suffering's embrace.[39]

Christian discipleship is in significant measure a matter of growing into this embrace, a matter of learning

> the choice of finitude before God. Adulthood, thus construed, would be a matter of discovering that it is possible, without diminution of dignity, abdication of rationality, or loss of freedom, to yield to what we know and be commanded by it. Such discovery would, nonetheless, be both dark and painful, for its pattern was set in the garden of Gethsemane.[40]

| | |

Respect for the Gift of Life

This does not mean that the suffering and death that afflict us and eventually steal our lives are themselves in any way goods or that we are to pursue them; to the contrary, it is *life* and *health* that are goods. And because life and health are goods, our lives and the lives of others are to be *respected*. The Christian is called to respect life not because life as such is an absolute good (that would be, after all, but a somewhat more nuanced version of the idolatry we are arguing against here) but that it always and everywhere comes from God and belongs to God.[41] The recognition that life belongs to God calls upon us to treat it as a "loan and a blessing"; such an understanding of life requires of us certain things.[42]

First, the recognition that life is a loan and a blessing requires the recognition that life is also in some sense a mystery. Respect for life thus "means an adoption of the distance proper in the face of a mystery. As such it must always be honoured with new wonder."[43] This insistence is certain to sound strange to modern ears, for we are increasingly persuaded that life is not a matter of mystery but of chemistry. Contemporary culture may on occasion and in its own way still honor life, but at the same time it drives the progressive deciphering and manipulation of life by an increasingly reductive science and a radically commercialized utilitarian technocracy. In some sense, recent gestures toward grand clinical applications in human genetics (for example) and the contemporary faith and health movement are but two sides of a single coin bearing an inscription promising the eventual mastery of life by two different varieties of human industry. Just so, both movements bear along with themselves the possibility of idolatry, in that they both permit and—however unrealistically—encourage the arbitrary dismissal of finitude. The frontiers of life, Barth reminds us, "must not be arbitrarily advanced in any spirit of frivolity or pedantry; they can be only reached in obedience and then respected as such."[44] To respect life means to treat its admittedly plastic limits "with holy awe."[45]

The recognition of life as loan and blessing requires also the maintenance of a profound awareness of the mutual interdependence of all life. "The grace that is the health of creatures," says Wendell Berry, "can only be held in common."[46] The New Testament reminder that our lives are not altogether our own is a description not simply of our relation to God but also of our relation to one another. In claiming that "man's creaturely existence as such is not his property; it is a loan [to be] held in trust," Barth intends to remind us that we ought to live as if our lives are loans or gifts not only *from God* but also to *each other*.[47] We flourish, in the fullest sense, only when and as those around us flourish; those others flourish fully only as we flourish. "My own life," Barth explains, "can no more claim my respect than that of others, but neither can that of others. Although they are not the same, but each distinct, the homogeneity and solidarity of all human life is indissoluble."[48]

Precisely because life is held in common, the presence of sickness or disability in our lives does not necessarily preclude our living well. We may agree with Barth that there is in *some sense* a universal human will to be free from illness, and we may also provisionally accept his definition of health, that it is "the strength to be as man," serving "human existence in the form of the capacity, vitality and freedom to exercise the psychical and physical functions, just as these themselves are only functions of human existence."[49] But we must also go with Barth beyond these claims to acknowledge that this capacity is not necessarily destroyed by sickness. For "sickness as such is not necessarily impotence to be as man. The strength to be this, so long as one is still alive, can also be the strength and therefore the health of the sick person."[50]

Sickness and health and the disabilities or abilities that accompany those states are, considered from the perspective of the isolated individual, always relative terms; if health suggests the capacity to do for oneself and sickness dependence on others, then none of us is ever healthy. The "strength to be as man" is not equivalent to independence, for we are all fundamentally dependent. It is given to each person at various times to bear the burdens of others' conspicuous dependence; it is likewise given to many of us at various times to have others bear the burdens of our own dependences. There is, as Alasdair MacIntyre says, "a scale of disability on which we all find ourselves. Disability is a matter of more or less, both in respect of degree of disability and in respect of the time periods in which we are disabled. And at different periods of our lives we find ourselves, often unpredictably, at very different points on that scale."[51]

|||

Sickness and Sin

By drawing attention to the interdependence of creatures and to the relative nature of our abilities and disabilities, we do not intend to belittle the sociopolitical or existential difficulties associated with serious illness. Indeed, if we are properly to respect life by acknowledging it as a loan and a blessing, we must, finally, acknowledge that at some level there exists a fundamental connection between our hatred of sickness and our efforts against it and our terror in the face of death. This connection, moreover, always involves confronting the complex and illusive connection between sickness and sin. If we are to respect life as loan and blessing, we must at least acknowledge this connection.

On some level this connection is intuitive. When we become sick, we ask questions about causes, and we often wonder whether we have done some specific thing to merit our illness. This wondering is in part the product of our understanding the biblical depiction of the connection, an understanding that is not altogether unjustified. There is, says Barth, a sense in which the biblical narrative depicts sickness as "a forerunner and messenger of death, and indeed of death as the judgment of God and the merited subjection of man to the power of nothingness in virtue of his sin."[52] But to say even this is not to claim, at least not necessarily, that any one person's particular history of alienation from God is the cause of his or her particular illnesses. Certainly there are suggestions in the biblical narrative that this *can* be the case, but there are also clear statements to the contrary.

A significant part of Jesus' teaching concerning human suffering in fact seems to be directed against the very idea of a direct causal relationship between individual sin and individual suffering. When the disciples asked him about the cause of a particular man's blindness, they presumed, as we often continue to do, that the man or someone close to him had *done something* to merit blindness: "Rabbi," they asked, "who sinned, this man or his parents, that he was born blind?" Jesus' complex response—in its own way nearly as disturbing as the disciples' assumption—seems designed, among other things, to dispel them of their belief in sin as the efficient cause of illness. "Neither this man nor his parents sinned; he was born blind so that God's works might be revealed in him."[53] What was apparently significant about the man, from Jesus' perspective, was not that he had done something that had led him to be blind but that because of the conspicuous way in which he had been affected by the universal human phenomenon of sin—his blindness—he had been excluded from participation in the life of God with the people of Israel.[54]

This suggests that the association of sin with sickness and death is not properly one of blunt, simple causation. There is a sense in which sickness and death, like the broad category sin itself, are manifestations of life in a creation that has not yet fully come into its own, not yet fully become what by the grace and power of God in Christ it is to be. Sickness is always *related* to sin, in that, like sin, "it is an element of the power of the chaos threatening creation on the one hand, and on the other an element and sign of God's righteous wrath and judgment, in short, an element and sign of the objective corruption which is related and corresponds to human sin and from which there is no deliverance apart from Jesus Christ."[55] Sin affects every fiber of the creation, irrespective of any given fiber's particular participation in this or that sinful action or inaction at any given time; likewise sickness is apt to be manifest at any time in any given creature, and this without apparent respect to the extent to which that creature has participated or is participating at that time in the creation's alienation from God. God has in the cross and resurrection of Christ overcome sin, but that victory is not yet fully manifest. The best of people still become sick, and all people still die, and we are not likely to get particular answers to our asking why this is the case.

| | |

The Christian Struggle against Sickness

This is not a modernized Stoic fatalism but a kind of theological realism. Sickness is not inevitable, and it is not always permanent, and Christians should not by default simply treat it as such. To the contrary, because life is a loan and a blessing, because it is God's good gift, whatever threatens it is to be fought against—but in proper measure and in particular ways.[56] There is extensive precedent for this claim: the church father Basil the Great, in his *Long Rules*, offers a starting place for Christians to discern properly both the measure and means of their struggle against illness:

> And when we were commanded to return to the earth whence we had been taken and were united with the pain ridden flesh doomed to destruction because of sin and, for the same reason, also subject to disease, the medical art was given to us to relieve the sick, in some degree at least. . . . Whatever requires an undue amount of thought or trouble or involves a large expenditure of effort and causes our whole life to revolve, as it were, around solicitude for the flesh must be avoided by Christians.[57]

Clearly Basil's claims here are made in conversation with a complex tradition. A good deal of Jesus' life may be characterized as a fight against sickness, and the apostolic church followed him by "being engaged in conflict against sickness and not at peace with it."[58] And so the contemporary church should likewise be expected to join the fight. In joining that fight, however, Christians are called to remember that they are fighting for a subordinate good. "For health, like life in general, is not an eternal but a temporal and therefore a limited possession."[59] Human life, in spite of its plasticity, has proper limits, and the transgression of those limits is potentially idolatry.[60]

Now typically when we make a statement of this sort with respect to human life and illness (that the transcendence of life's proper limits is idolatry), we do so with reference to whether it is proper to us as creatures to use this or that technology to extend or improve the circumstances of life. Such uses, however, are only displays of a more fundamental disposition, a possible refusal to live as if our lives—indeed, as if *every* life—are finite and temporal, as if they belong to God and are therefore to be lived as loans and blessings. When we imagine, however tacitly, however implicitly, that God exists to give us what we want, to extend our lives and increase our vigor and always and everywhere to deliver us now from sickness and suffering, we imagine a deity other than the one present to the world in Jesus of Nazareth. Only as we do not seek to constrain God by demanding freedom from finitude do we live before and in worship of a God who is perfectly free; only as we live before and in worship of such a God are we free to live as human creatures. And this requires that we receive and pursue health as the limited and subordinate good that it is.

This is finally the meaning of respect for life, that we reserve for God the ultimate right to determine its proper course and limits. And doing this is more than simply praying "Thy will be done." "For the life of man belongs to him. He has granted it to him as a loan. And he decides in what its right use should consist. He also decrees and decides . . . in what man's will to live should at any moment consist or not, and how far it should go or not go as such."[61] Just so, the Christian struggle against sickness and death never confuses efficacy with faithfulness. Sickness is to be fought against, even to the point of death, but God is not to be resisted. The distinction is a subtle one that is difficult and perhaps sometimes impossible to discern. "There is still no question of capitulation to sickness, far less to the realm of death manifested in it. But there is certainly capitulation to God who is the Lord even of sickness and the realm of death, and is gracious to man even in the fact that he permits him to fall sick, to be sick and perhaps even to die of sickness."[62]

This of course requires not simply faithfulness, which can be borne along for a time by religious enthusiasm, but also enthusiasm's partner, which is patience. Patience gives to faithfulness its own inherent effectiveness, for patience is not to be confused here with Stoic apathy or with the self-deceptive passivity characteristic of the religion that Marx called the opiate of the masses. It is something altogether different.

> Again, there is not a question of giving up the will for health and the fight against sickness. But there is certainly a full and true readiness to become and be well exclusively through and for God, which must necessarily consist in quiet endurance of the present and perhaps tri-

umphant sickness. Strictly speaking, therefore, the necessary aug-
mentation of what we have already said can consist only in the recol-
lection that, if this fight is to be fought rightly and finally, it will not
exclude but include patience. Sickness in so far as it is still present, the
impairing, disturbing and destroying of life in so far as these are an
event and cannot be removed by faith and prayer . . . have therefore to be "borne" in the sense that they are drawn by God – who is
present in this way, too, as Lord and Victor—into what he wills from
and with man, and what in its entirety, because it comes from Him,
cannot be evil but only good, and cannot be pain but only joy.[63]

This strange insistence, that God is present "as Lord and Victor" *even
as sickness and death seem to triumph*, evokes one of the great challenges of
Christian discipleship, which is *to live* as if God is present, "as Lord and
Victor," even in the midst of horrible circumstances, including sickness,
suffering, and death. This is not a matter of passivity or nonresistance to
the evils that are sickness, suffering, and death, but one of a *particular
kind* of resistance. What distinguishes Christian patience from Stoic apathy or idealist fatalism is the Christian eschatological hope. Christian
patience is eschatological patience. It is a curious interweaving of antici-
patory waiting—for the final establishment of a reign of God in which
there will be neither sickness nor suffering nor death—with a confident
freedom from terror in the face of those awful (un)realities. This interweaving produces a curious, richly textured fabric, from which the Christian community may tailor the garments it wears into its battle against
suffering.

| | |

Garments for Battle: The Apocalyptic
Struggle against Illness

To speak of garments for battle and of the embrace of suffering in anticipation of final victories over various kinds of evil is to enter into the
strange and for the most part overlooked language and world of apocalyptic. By apocalyptic, we mean simply the notion that God has revealed
to the gathered community of God's people the particular and unex-
pected ways in which God is redemptively at work in their midst. It has
been an assumption of much theology in the modern era that apocalyptic, because it belonged to a more primitive time and was the instrument
of an unsophisticated, oppressed minority community, is in modernity
best dismissed, or at least explained away. But this is a mistake, for if we

are to speak faithfully about matters of sickness and death and of faithful Christian dispositions and actions toward them, we must speak that language and adopt what David Toole has called an "apocalyptic style."[64]

The first task of learning this language and of adopting this style—that is, this way of life—is a task of the moral imagination; Christians must craft imaginations capable of seeing and living in a world in which God is, in spite of every evidence to the contrary, redemptively present and active. This is not to deny the sometimes fantastic, always metaphorical character of apocalyptic language but to suggest that such language is a necessary aspect of learning to see, speak about, and live in a world in which God is active in ways invisible to the untrained eye. As John Howard Yoder explains:

> The substantial assumption that moves the [apocalyptic] seer is that God is an actor. *How* God acts can be expressed only in metaphors which our mechanically formed vision can only consider fantastic or poetic. Nonetheless, the addressees of "revelation" are expected or commanded to behave differently, *within* the system of the real world, because of that information which has been "disclosed" to them about God as a purposeful actor.[65]

To possess an imagination so formed is far from natural. We eschew apocalyptic language, in part because we associate it with terror and horrific endings but also because we find the very idea that God works outside what we believe are the normal patterns of cause and effect virtually untenable.[66] We are much more comfortable, especially as we live on this side of the scientific revolution, with the idea that God works in ways that are natural and scientifically verifiable. In our time, it is not unusual—nor is it inappropriate—for people of faith to pray that God would work in and through the hands of medical caregivers or that God would multiply the activity or ensure the effectiveness of some broadly accepted therapeutic agent. But this is not, if the biblical narrative is to be believed, the sole or maybe even the primary mode of God's action in the world. It is precisely the difference of the biblical world that challenges us at this point, asking us to imagine another way. The biblical story "inserts into our present setting a fulcrum capable of being leaned on to pry us away from the assumption that the world as we see it is the only way it can be."[67]

As a way of thinking and speaking about God's presence and action in history, apocalyptic encourages us to discern and identify God's presence and action in ways and places that may not readily be associated with therapeutic spirituality. We learn from the biblical story that God's presence and action are best represented not by the modern worldview's "massive causal nexus with no loopholes"[68] but by the promise of the prophet Isaiah, who exhorted Israel *in the midst of* her collapse at the hands of a foreign military power: "Do not fear, for I have redeemed you; I have called you by name, you are mine. When you pass through the waters, I will be with you; and through the rivers, they shall not overwhelm you; when you walk through the fire you shall not be burned, and the flame will not consume you."[69] Such presence and action are seen paradigmatically in the life and teachings of Jesus of Nazareth, for the peculiar politics and the decidedly apocalyptic style of Jesus brings into sharp relief the contrast between effectiveness and faithfulness.

The faithfulness required by apocalyptic does not in every case entail the abandonment of effectiveness, and it never entails resignation or the abandonment of hope. Rather, it expands hope, giving it a place outside the realm of effectiveness. In the apocalyptic idiom, "the key to the obedience of God's people is not their effectiveness, but their patience."[70] Just so, what faithfulness does entail is the abandonment of the need to control outcomes by manipulating antecedent events that may or may not be causal. For Christians, the model of faithfulness is Jesus, who "rejects the temptation to grab hold of a handle on history and to move events in 'the right direction.' He refuses that kind of power and that kind of kingship that finds its support in violence; and he opts instead to resist just this kind of power by going to the cross."[71] In his refusal to manipulate the circumstances of his confrontation with power Jesus did not abdicate responsibility; rather, he implied that responsibility involves discerning that history ultimately works in ways that are not always apparent.[72] History, says Yoder, works according to a different logic, and "the relationship between the obedience of God's people and the triumph of God's cause is not a relationship of cause and effect but one of cross and resurrection."[73]

This is of course the ultimate, scandalous paradox of Christianity. In and through the murder of Jesus, in and through his subjection to and his free acceptance of a slave's death, God triumphs over evil:

> Thus it is that the author of Colossians can declare that in Jesus and through the cross, God "disarmed the principalities and powers and made a public example of them, triumphing over them in him [or 'it']" (Colossians 2:15). The image is that of a victory parade like those the Romans sometimes staged after a major success in war. And as Wink notes, "the most exciting part of the parade was dragging the defeated enemy through the streets and exposing them to

public ridicule. To say God triumphed over the principalities and powers is to say that he paraded them before the world as captives in their defeat; it is also to say that he defeated them precisely by thus exposing them. Indeed, the Greek term *apekdysamenos*, translated as "disarmed," conveys the sense of "stripping off" or "undressing": the image is that of armor coming off. The overarching message of Colossians 2:15, then, is that God defeated the powers by "exposing" them. "Exposure" is the theme that runs throughout the entire verse; and the punch line is that Jesus exposed the Powers at the cross.[74]

The claim that Jesus exposed and made an example of the forces that killed him even in the midst of and through that killing suggests an analogy, namely, that there may be instances in which the enemies that are illness, suffering, and death may be exposed and made an example of even as they remain thoroughly entrenched features of a given life and appear to be triumphing over that life. The frequent appearance of the imagery of the cross in New Testament accounts of discipleship and the fact that Jesus told those who followed him on more than one occasion that their discipleship would involve "taking up" a cross suggests that a proper Christian disposition toward suffering, including the suffering that is due to illness, is built on a cross-shaped foundation.

This is not to deny that there are definite limits to the analogy between the forces that brought about Jesus' suffering and those we think of as being responsible for our own. The cross, an instrument of Roman imperial terror, is not an appropriate cipher for every form or instance of human suffering. The distinction, as Yoder sees it, is one of agency: the sufferings of Jesus were intended by the agents of the Roman Empire and voluntarily taken on by Jesus of Nazareth.

> The cross of Christ was not an inexplicable or chance event, which happened to strike him, like illness or accident. To accept the cross as his destiny, to move toward it and even provoke it, when he could well have done otherwise, was Jesus' constantly reiterated free choice; and he warns his disciples lest their embarking on the same path be less conscious of its costs."[75]

Yet Yoder goes too far, in our estimation, when he denies the very possibility that suffering due to sickness can be an aspect of faithfulness if it is endured in the light of Christ's endurance of the cross. The comparison is legitimate, so long as it remains metaphorical. This means, as Wendell Berry has written, that it must be "controlled by a sort of humorous intelligence, always mindful of the exact limits within which the comparison is being made."[76] By this standard, Yoder's own characterization of the cross of Christ and the similar fates of his disciples appears to allow room for such a limited comparison. He notes that "the early Christians had to be warned against claiming merit for any and all suffering; only if their suffering be innocent, and a result of the evil will of their adversaries, may it be understood as meaningful before God."[77] We have already called attention to the oblique and largely inscrutable nature of the relation of illness to sin; seldom, if ever, can we say that a particular instance of illness is deserved in the sense that it has been brought about by specific sins of the sick person. Job's question remains unanswered, and in this sense, at least, a good deal of our suffering due to illness is "innocent." Just so, the cross as a symbol of Jesus' acceptance and performance of suffering might serve as a significant lens through which Christians may view their own suffering due to illness.[78]

Of course, such a lens is neither an explanation nor an antidote for suffering. "There is," says Stanley Hauerwas, "no hope for us if our only hope on the face of suffering is that 'we can learn from it,' or that we can use what we learn from the treatment of that suffering to overcome eventually what has caused it . . or that we can use suffering to organize our energies to mount effective protests against oppression."[79] Neither is seeing Christian suffering due to illness through the lens of the cross simply a way of compensating for or staving off the despair that inevitably comes when all other forms of intervention into illness fail. Rather, it is paradigmatic way of displaying the Christian virtue of hope, a virtue that is rooted in the fact that God's ultimate response to the cross was to vindicate Jesus' suffering by raising him from the dead.

Yoder remarks that the "biblical seers were not compensating for desperation—at least they did not say they were. They said they were engaging in doxology, restating in a different setting their proclamation of the resurrection. They were testifying that the powers of oppression were swallowed up in God's larger story, whereas our modern explanations try to do it the other way 'round, by subsuming God talk in our own visions of human dignity and therapy."[80] Thus the resurrection, which Yoder elsewhere says is nothing less than God's vindication of Jesus' decision to endure the suffering of the cross, is for Christians the signal event in history.[81] The resurrection is the rest of the story of the cross, and so completes our most fundamental assumption about who God is and how God works in the world. Suffering may be endured because the death it foretells has lost its sting. It has been swallowed up in the power of the resurrection; in the resurrected Jesus, we see "the *form* of death (the marks of crucifixion) without its content. What is given . . . is not only the particular act of God in the case of Jesus, of loving him through and beyond the barrier of death, but the permanent way in which God has made death an empty threat; his gratuitous, loving presence is always present as overcoming death at any given moment."[82]

The power of the resurrection may be manifest in the present age in a variety of ways; we dare not attempt to place limits on God's goodness.[83] Yet most if not all the ways that power is displayed are political, in that they require the presence of a community that bears witness to God's work in the world. For the alternative, apocalyptic reality of the resurrection, and so the triumph of Jesus through the cross, is apprehended and displayed only by faith, and faith is formed and sustained in the alternative politics of a concrete material community. We must begin to describe such a community and the ways it makes possible the hope and patience that sustain those who suffer as they await resurrection; it is to this task that we turn in our final chapter.

Satisfying Our Eager Longing

Toward a Christian Politics of Sickness, Healing, and Caring

And I tell you I saw there a cross with a man nailed
to it, silvery in the mist, and I said to him: "Are you
*   the Christ?" And he must have heard me, for in his*
agony, twisted as he was, he nodded his head affirmatively,
*   up and down, once and twice. And a little way off*
I saw another cross with another man nailed to it,
*   twisting and nodding, and then another and another,*
ranks and divisions of crosses straggling like exhausted
*   legions upward among the misty trees, each cross*
with a silvery, writhing, twisting, nodding, naked
*   figure nailed to it, and some of them were women.*
The hill was filled with crucifixion. Should I not be
*   telling you this? Is it excessive? But I know something*
about death now, I know how silent it is, silent even
*   when the pain is shrieking and screaming. And tonight*
is very silent and very dark. . . .

HAYDEN CARRUTH

When we've lost it all, we've had what we've lost.

WENDELL BERRY

*   the wages of goodness*
are oblique and obscure, and not even assured.

MICHAEL BLUMENTHAL

Our world can be a hard and sometimes dark place, and sickness and death tend only to make it harder and darker. When we find ourselves in such a hard place, "when the pain is shrieking and screaming," when it "is very silent and dark,"[1] we seek solace wherever we can find it. We turn in such times to God, hoping to gain his ear, hoping to be delivered from, or at least comforted in, our suffering. And surely it is not wrong for Christians to do this, to turn to God for solace. It is not wrong to seek health, to pray for healing and for deliverance, and to rejoice when they come, for these things are all God's good gifts, and our tradition reminds us that we are not simply permitted but even fervently commanded to seek them.[2] Health is among the most basic goods, not just of the Christian life but of all life; not just for the sake of the individual but also for the sake of those many others for whom she is called to be healthy. We seek life and health because they are requisite to our being servants, especially to those who lack them. Yet we are mistaken if we demand that God heal us, acting as if health is among our inalienable rights. Something has gone wrong when we expect that health should be ours *because* we faithfully and sincerely make supplication to God.

It is not wrong to beseech God to remove our suffering or extend our lives or magnify our vigor. But we err if we act as if that is mainly what God is *for*. And we are, perhaps most important, simply mistaken if we abandon hope when suffering continues or health is illusory, or if we despair of God when sickness persists or death seems imminent. For Christians, these are not conclusions but starting places. The hard work of Christian discipleship begins here, in the face of the difficult task of negotiating life as mortal and broken bodies in a finite and broken world, and of doing so without losing hope.

The Christian cannot escape or ignore that even after the resurrection, in which he stands victorious over death, Jesus of Nazareth is the Lamb of God who stands always "as if it had been slaughtered."[3] God is the *first* among those many "twisting, nodding, naked" figures nailed to crosses in our distance. And so it is in some sense *from* that cross, even as God destroys the power of the evil for which it stands, that God rules the cosmos and comforts or delivers the afflicted. To realize this is to understand that within the horizon of this life, the course of Christian fidelity has a complex relationship to the course of our desire for relief from suffering, sometimes overlapping, sometimes diverging, sometimes intersecting, seldom predictably, and always beyond easy control. When we are sick and suffering, or when the people we love are sick and suffering, deliverance may or may not be forthcoming. Moreover, we can never know in advance and probably cannot know in retrospect the precise relationship of our fervent prayers to the way things turn out. But the absence of deliverance from sickness or suffering is neither a sign that God has withdrawn favor nor an occasion to abandon hope. The God on the cross remains present *and* powerful, even when things seem to go horribly wrong, even when consolation seems unavailable.

It is not an easy thing to believe and to live as if this is so. Such living requires a faith that is learned from attending carefully to the witness of those who have endured the misery of intractable suffering and who still believe and are able and willing to speak of that belief. This is a skill, certainly, but it is also a grace. It is a gift, perhaps of the sort spoken of by the poet Donald Hall, who wrote the poems in the book *Without* to chronicle his wife Jane Kenyon's decline and death from leukemia. In one of those poems, he speaks of his feeling of helplessness standing at her bedside during a particularly acute stage of her illness, wanting to do something for her "when there was exactly nothing to do." Hall recounts his feelings at that moment by evoking an image familiar to anyone confronted, whether for the first time or the hundredth, by the fact that finally, his control over the things that might happen to him or those he loves is limited at least: "Inside him, / some four-year-old / understood that if he was good—thoughtful, / considerate, beyond / reproach, *perfect*—she would not leave him."[4]

Yet the familiar image of a controllable God who may be manipulated by devotion or exemplary behavior, a God who responds to human goodness by blessing it with security and happiness, does not have the last word in *Without*. In telling of the regular visits he and Kenyon received from their pastor, Hall offers a very different portrayal of God and a very different sense of the way God was with them during their suffering, as a presence that promised nothing but itself:

When their minister,
Alice Ling, brought communion to the house
Or the hospital bed,
Or when they held hands as Alice prayed,
Grace was evident
But not the comfort of mercy or reprieve.
The embodied figure
On the cross still twisted under the sun.[5]

This is a mysterious and difficult grace, this grace that is clearly evident but that may not include "the comfort of mercy or reprieve." What, we must ask, does it mean to experience such grace, to know a God who was present with us and those whom we love, in sickness and suffering, even as "The embodied figure / On the cross still twisted under the sun?" Put differently, what does it mean to trust in the presence, and ultimately in the redemption, offered by a crucified God who continues to have the appearance of a Lamb that has been slaughtered?

| | |
Hope between Tragedy and Comedy

Just because it is so particular and so difficult to achieve, the grace that is the Christian practice of experiencing God's presence in suffering demands the rejection of two rather simplistic extremes. On the one hand, as we have said repeatedly, we must abandon the notion that God can or should be controlled by our behavior. God may not be domesticated within any variety of expectation that our devotion will be rewarded or responded to as an effect following a cause. The bluntly comedic belief that a life lived under the protection of God's grace *necessarily* includes the blessings, eventual or immediate, that are health or deliverance from suffering in simple exchange for devotion has little to do with Christianity. It is instead a strange synthesis of capitalist ideology, modern self-help doctrine, and the same caricatured Deuteronomic theology against which Jesus so frequently argued.

We must also, on the other hand, avoid the tragic extreme of plunging into despair, believing that because relief from suffering is not immediately forthcoming, there is no comfort and God has abandoned us to our suffering. It is a prominent theme, not simply in the Christian tradition but also in certain strands of the Hebrew scriptures, that the righteous often suffer, the wicked often prosper, and "the wages of goodness are oblique and obscure, and not even assured." Yet none of this is reason for despair; for even when we can only, as the poet Michael Blumenthal writes, "keep singing into the light of this darkening world," we can, at least, do that.[6] Singing, after all, is way of making a case for and cultivating the virtue of hope. And hope is essential if we are to complete our journey along an arduous path toward an eternal destination that is attainable only with God's help.[7]

Hope is a necessary virtue just *because* the journey of life is arduous. As we reject despair and domestication, neither can we embrace as the Christian way a neatly tooled compromise that fits cleanly between these extremes. The "blessed hope" that constitutes the Christian promise is not simply an eschatological middle way between tragedy and comedy, not simply an abandonment of hope in this life in favor of a premature rush toward the better conditions of the next. Life in the world to come is certainly real, but it by no means entails a rejection of or hurrying through this life or this world. Because life in this complex, dense, and fleshy world is God's good gift, the Christian hope for fullness of life is forever complex, dense, and fleshy.

For a sense of the shape this hope might take in unhappy times, we may turn to the shared life of an imagined people who have known and lived such hope and among whom it is prominently displayed. The novel *A Place on Earth* is the cornerstone of Wendell Berry's extended fictional account of the lives of the inhabitants of a rural Kentucky town whom Berry calls the "Port William membership." At the center of *A Place on Earth* is the household of Mat and Margaret Feltner, whose families have lived and worked, primarily as farmers, for generations in Port William. As the story begins, sometime in the early days of World War II, we learn that the Feltners' daughter-in-law, Hannah, is living with Mat and Margaret. Hannah is married to the Feltners' son, Virgil, who is serving in the army, and she is pregnant. From the book's opening scene we are shown clearly that the war represents an especially severe intrusion on the membership. It has disrupted their lives, and especially the life of the Feltner household. Yet we also see that the membership is a people devoted to living as best they can no matter what the circumstances, doing the same good work they and their forebears have been doing for years. It is their devotion to their work and their devotion to one another and their devotion to Port William, we sense, that sustains their anticipation that life will someday resume its normal rhythms; hard times come and go, and the members sustain one another in the midst of both. The Feltners' anticipation that their present hard times will soon pass is tested, however, when they receive a letter indicating that something awful has happened:

> Mat goes to the table and holds the letter out to Hannah. There comes over him a great need to do this gently. But he can only do it bluntly, with a kind of shame as though there might be a polite way to do it but he does not know what it is.
>
> She reaches out for the letter and takes it. Mat knows she is looking at him, but he does not look at her. And he knows when she looks away from him. She tears open the envelope and reads the letter, and lays it slowly and flatly down on the table, indicating that Mat should read it. And Mat reads it, and then, as though the duty falls to him, he reads aloud: "Virgil Feltner . . . missing in action."[8]

The family and those close to them are of course terribly distressed by this news. They are tempted to fear the worst, to think that Virgil is dead. Yet they refuse to cultivate that fear. They simply will not allow it to linger, forcing themselves instead to hope that he is alive and that everything will eventually be all right. They continue to live their lives as best they can, perhaps—by sheer force of will—even more "normally" than before the news arrived. But their hope is clearly become strained, and as a strained hope it can be sustained for only so long. As the story proceeds, the tension created by their wondering about Virgil's fate increases and begins to weigh heavily, especially on Mat. Time passes, and life goes on: the Feltners and their neighbors plant, tend, and harvest crops. Members of the community continue periodically to gather and scatter, eating and drinking, celebrating and mourning as the occasion demands. Eventually, the Feltners' granddaughter is born. Yet through all this, Mat is unable to escape the pressing sense that the passing of time only increases the likelihood that Virgil is dead.

As the family's concern and sorrow grows, it spreads to their friends and neighbors, and this plight results, as it so often does in the small towns of the rural South, in a visit from the well-intentioned young pastor of the community church. As something of an outsider, he is clearly uncomfortable with the task of comforting the Feltners, who are respected and usually stalwart pillars of the community. In his discomfort, he feels he must *say* something—something that will be helpful to them. The family gathers in the parlor, and for a time they make small talk. But as soon as there is a lull in the conversation, the minister begins. "My friends," he says, "I've come because I know of your trouble," and then begins to speak, "fleeing into the safe coherence of his own words," of a hope that "rides above all chances of mortal and worldly hope, hastening to rest in the hope of Heaven."

The preacher's commendation of hope in a life to come, an ethereal hope "in which all the riddles and ends of the world are gathered, illuminated, and bound," is one that Mat, at least, is unable or unwilling to embrace. For although it promises a kind of freedom from the cares of the world that is in a certain way pleasant, Mat recognizes that it also abandons to hopelessness the good gift that is this life in this world. It occurs to him that

> In this hope—this last simplifying rest-giving movement of the mind—Mat realizes that he is not free, and never has been. He is doomed to hope in the world, in the bonds of his own love. He is doomed to take every chance and desperate hope of hope between him and death, Virgil's, Margaret's, his. His hope of Heaven must be the hope of a man bound to the world that his life is not ultimately futile or ultimately meaningless, hope more burdening than despair.
>
> It is from this possibility of meaninglessness that the preacher has retreated. So that the earth will not be plunged into the darkness, he has lifted up the Heavenly City and hastened to refuge in its gates. And Mat, in the very act of leaning toward that restfulness, turns away from it to take back his pain.[9]

Mat cannot abide a hope that is dismissive of this life and this world, and so he forces himself to embrace a painful alternative. He hopes in a world that, because it is filled with pain as well as beauty, contains within itself the very real possibility of hopelessness, the possibility of its own failure. For a time, he is able to tolerate the pain he reclaims, bearing its considerable burden alone, as if he can simply *will* himself to go on and perhaps even will Virgil to return. But then, a day comes when grief outgrows hope and becomes determinative of Mat's world. He can no longer keep his thoughts to himself. As he sits one afternoon on the porch with his wife and his daughter-in-law and her baby, he is compelled to speak his mind:

> Margaret shifts the baby down onto her lap. She lies there quietly, wide eyed.
>
> "Won't Virgil be proud of her when he comes back!" Margaret says, her voice resonant with the thought.
>
> And an anger begins in Mat that he seems to have been waiting for, and that he welcomes. "Don't, Margaret."
>
> He speaks quietly, making an effort to do so, but his voice tightens and hardens with his anger. "Don't talk like that any more. That's not doing us any good."
>
> The two women look at him.
>
> It is not until then that he fully realizes what he has to say. A kind of panic hits him, a kind of sickness. But his words are empowered by anger as they never could have been by grief.
>
> "Virgil is dead. He's not going to come back. He's dead, Margaret. Hannah, he's dead. Say so."
>
> He gets up, and without looking at them again goes out the back door.
>
> "So be it," he tells himself. "It had to be."[10]

Mat's confrontation with the harsh truth of Virgil's death is at first cathartic, in that it enables his mourning. Soon, however, mourning gives way to a sort of lonely resignation to the tragedy that is the loss of a beloved son. His presentation of naked truth to Margaret and Hannah gives birth to a new kind of sorrow that descends over the household. We come to sense at times that these are people who have seen the horrible truth that the rest of us fear: that the world is without purpose and life without meaning. Such sorrow could easily plunge them into despair, yet it does not, for they are able, somehow, to achieve a new and different and ultimately better hope. The hope they achieve is at once strange and beautiful; it is articulated most clearly by Margaret one evening as they once again sit quietly together on the porch. She asks her husband, "What are you thinking about, Mat?" to which he replies, despondently, if not a bit self-pityingly, "Loss . . . Loss. It singles us out."

But Margaret, sad though she is, does not altogether share Mat's sentiment, and she does not allow his claim to go unchallenged. For her experience of loss is a different one.

> "Mat, when we've lost it all, we've *had* what we've lost."
>
> "But to *lose* it. Isn't there anything in you that rebels against that?"
>
> She looks steadily at him, considering that—whether unsure of her answer or unwilling to answer too readily, he cannot tell. He is aware that Margaret is trying him, drawing deliberately at the bindings between them, as he has tried her with his singleness.
>
> "No," she says.
>
> "None at all?"
>
> "Virgil," she says, as if to remind or acknowledge what they are talking about. "From the day he was born I knew he would die. That was how I loved him, partly. I'd brought him into the world that would give him things to love, and take them away. You, too, Mat. You knew it. I knew so well that he would die that, when he did disappear from us the way he did, I was familiar with the pain. I'd had it in me all his life."

It is significant, we think, that the view to which Margaret gives voice in this scene is not a romanticized nihilism. It is not an aesthetically praiseworthy despair. Her longstanding grasp of the reality that Virgil would someday die is part of her broader understanding that all life is filled with painful loss. It has been bearable because it has been accompanied by the recognition, cultivated along with her understanding that loss is part of life, that loss is painful precisely because it stands in stark comparison to the tremendous joy that comes from receiving life as the purposeful and plenteous gift of a gracious Creator. Margaret has learned over the years the art of cultivating that spirit of gratitude that is the foundation of the virtue of hope. Moments later, at the conclusion of the same scene, she continues:

> "But I don't believe that when his death is subtracted from his life it leaves nothing. Do you, Mat?"
>
> "No," he says, "I don't."
>
> "What it leaves is his life. How could I turn away from it now any more than I could when he was a little child, and not love it and be glad of it, just because death is in it?"

Her words fall on him like water and like light. Suffering and clarified, he feels himself made fit for her by what she asks of him. He shakes his head.

She is clearly asking him now, and he gets up and goes and sits down beside her. He puts his arm around her.

"And Mat," she say, "we belong to each other. After all these years. Doesn't that mean something?"

It is a long time before he answers. The night has nearly come. He can see only the drifting white blur of Hannah's blouse under the dark hovering of the tree.

"I don't know what it means," he says finally. "I know what it's worth."[11]

The Feltners' capacity, to face, endure, and thrive in spite of pain and suffering is a difficult grace. And although we admit to being speculative at this point, we think it fair to say that such a grace can only be acquired as part of an entire way of life. The center of that acquisition is a shared life in a particular kind of community. It is such a common life that makes a household like the Feltners' and a community of households like Port William. One of the lessons Mat learns over the course of the story is that he is unable to bear the pain of his son's disappearance alone; rather, such pain can only be borne in the midst of and with the help of others who are likewise committed to sharing a certain kind of love as part of the entirety of their life together.

In this remarkable story we are presented with gestures toward three distinct possibilities of responding to suffering and loss: a tragic despair, a comedic, too-hurried fleeing from this life to the next, and the hard work that is the joyful-painful embrace of one another in this life, in the assurance that its worth is founded by the God who has experienced and overcome loss in the cross and resurrection. We believe that only the third is consistent with the richness of the Christian tradition and its healing presence to sickness and suffering.

| | |

A Religion of Healing—But What Kind?

If the broad task of faithfulness in and toward sickness and suffering is characterized by the virtue of hope, the great challenge for contemporary Christians, especially in the face of the rise of the faith and health movement, is to describe in concrete terms what it means to embody the tradition that the great historian of Christianity Adolf von Harnack called "the religion of salvation or healing."[12] It is not precisely clear what Harnack meant by this description of *ancient* Christianity, much less that of the twenty-first century. Clearly the claim is predicated to a significant extent on the gospel depictions of Jesus repeatedly performing miracles of healing and exorcism.[13] Yet to suggest that because Jesus performed miracles of healing, women and men have come to Christianity through the centuries *for* healing is to distort the place of healing in the New Testament and the subsequent Christian tradition.

> There is no doubt that miracles of healing are assigned a central place in the ministry of Jesus by the writers of the Gospels, who consistently portray them as a manifestation of the presence of the Kingdom of God. The miracles are not, however, viewed by the Evangelists as an end in themselves. Rather, they represent the external aspect of salvation, the physical manifestation of a new spiritual order. The vocabulary of the Gospels (both the Synoptic Gospels and the Fourth Gospel) is revealing. The healings performed by Jesus are spoken of as "signs" that bear witness to his messianic credentials; and they are regarded as the fulfillment of messianic prophecies contained in the Hebrew Scriptures (see, e.g., Matt. 11:4–5, which echoes Isa. 35:4–6 and 61:1). Thus Matthew 8:16–17 describes Jesus' ministry of healing and exorcism as a fulfillment of the prophecy of Isaiah 53:4 ("He took up our infirmities and carried our diseases"). Jesus himself is reported in the Fourth Gospel as citing his miracles as a sign of his messiahship (John 10:37–38; cf. Acts 2:22).[14]

So the church has always understood miraculous healing to have a place in the proclamation of the gospel message, but a place centering on healing being among the visible signs that a new social and political order, a new reign of God, has begun. This is not to deny that the Christian practice of healing has benefited those it has freed from sickness, for clearly it has. And it is not to deny that such benefits have been signs of that universal health to come, for they are, at least in part, precisely that. It is to suggest, rather, that a focus on the benefit for the individual is potentially distracting from the real focus of the Gospel, the Kingdom of God, and from Jesus, whose life was and is the embodied presence of the Kingdom in a concrete, historical person—the *autobasileia*, the "kingdom itself."[15] Subsequent to Jesus' resurrection and ascension to the right hand of the Father, the Kingdom remains present to the world by the power of the Spirit. The presence of the Kingdom is first of all in the gathered community's eucharistic celebration, and then in the community itself, as an extension of the fact that those gathered to eat and drink

Jesus' body and blood have themselves actually become God's presence to the world and understand themselves in precisely that way.[16] Thus the locus of the healing presence of Jesus in the world has become the community that gathers in his name. This suggests that the way the community is to embody its commitment to be a healing presence to sickness and suffering has to do first of all with politics—that is, with the way the community orders itself with respect to those who are sick and suffering. None of this is to say that Christians stopped (or should stop) praying for miraculous healing, or believing that God could and would miraculously heal, but that such healing was only one part of the broader Christian commitment to care for the sick, which is itself simply one aspect of the community's being the presence of the Kingdom to the world.[17]

Here Harnack was correct; from the beginning, the Christian commitment to the sick and suffering has been profound. Hector Avalos has suggested that Christianity from its earliest days constituted a "health care system," by which he means "a set of interacting resources, institutions, and strategies that are intended to maintain or restore health in a particular community."[18] And while Avalos, in our view, overestimates the role of miraculous healing in the rise of Christianity, he is certainly correct to insist that sickness and suffering were primary social and political concerns around which the early Christians organized their communities. Notwithstanding his allusion to utilitarian motives, the historian of medicine Guenter Risse makes this point quite clearly with regard to the very early church:

> Joining this religion ensured membership in a dedicated network of believers whose family values protected widows and orphans and whose nursing services were eagerly sought during earthquakes, fires, and epidemics. Christianity thus became the basis for a new social solidarity eminently suited to the periodic chaos afflicting urban dwellers.[19]

The primitive Christian concern for the sick and suffering persisted and developed as Christianity became better established in the ancient Mediterranean world. In the East, within just a few years of the time the church was permitted to own property, Christian houses of hospitality, called *xendocheion*, were opened to the sick. In the West, the monasteries of the Benedictine order were frequently places where the sick and dying received care. [20]

> Instead of the reciprocal hospitality that had prevailed in ancient Greece and the family-oriented obligations of the Romans, Chris-

tianity adopted ancient Egyptian and Jewish models of social welfare that targeted particular social groups marginalized by poverty, sickness, and age. Jewish communities had offered hostels to house the poor and sick travelers, and their healers were obligated to treat the sick poor. Houses were even set aside for lepers. Now Christians adopted similar responses to protect their own brethren.[21]

| | |

Resurrection, Inclusion, and Care

What we see here is a close connection between the Christian commitment to be with and to care for the sick and suffering and the Christian virtue of hospitality to the stranger.[22] This connection, moreover, suggests that those Christian practices associated with sickness and suffering take a form particular to certain of the theological commitments of the Christian tradition. For help on this point we may turn again to the story of Jesus' healing of the man born blind in the fourth Gospel. According to James Alison, this and all of the healing stories in the New Testament must be read through the lens of the resurrection of Jesus from the dead, the definitive sign that God's Kingdom has come and that it has triumphed over sin and all its effects. Just as the resurrection is the ultimate sign of the Kingdom and its victory over sin, sickness, and death, so are the healing stories incremental signs of that same victory. If we read the healing stories in this way, we gain a remarkable insight, not only into the typically inscrutable relationship of sickness and suffering to sin but also into the particular way that Jesus' presence truly "heals" in this life. Jesus heals, quite simply, by overcoming sin and the most significant of its effects, alienation. This suggests that the effect of sin implied and the healing depicted in the fourth gospel is politically, and not just personally, significant:

> The structure of what has happened is twofold: it is simultaneously that of an inclusion and an exclusion. In the first place, the story is of an inclusion. The man was blind from birth and also cut off not only from a certain participation in the human good, but also from full integration in the community of Israel. His blindness was considered part of a moral defect that meant he was ipso facto impure and unable to participate in the cultic life of Israel.[23]

Here the details are significant. The healing took place on the Sabbath, the day on which the man's exclusion from the life of the community would perhaps have been most conspicuously evident. Jesus used clay in the healing, and he mixed it with his own saliva; this may be a sign of his restoration of the original goodness of the material creation. Finally, the completion of the healing required the man to wash in a pool outside the wall of the city, and then to reenter the city with his vision intact. According to Alison, this washing and reentering represents the entrance into life in the new creation that is established through baptism; the man is not only restored to health as an individual but is also reincorporated by his washing into the Israel of God.[24]

Yet Jesus' offering the blind man the possibility of full membership and participation in the life of Israel is only one of the points made by the story. The story also offers "a revolution in the understanding of sin, a revolution that takes place around the life of Jesus but is actually worked out in the life of someone else."[25] After his healing, the man was presented to the religious leaders of the community, who, when they learned that their opponent, Jesus, had been the one by whose hand the man had regained his sight, expelled the man from the synagogue. Here we see not only sin of a determinatively political sort but also, in light of the life, death, and resurrection of Jesus, a fundamental rethinking of the connection between sickness and sin: "At the end of the tale sin is considered as the act of exclusion: the real blindness is the blindness which is not only present in those who exclude, but actually intensifies during the act of exclusion."[26] The real sin, in light of Jesus' establishment of the new, inclusive humanity that is citizenship in the Kingdom of God, is the sin of those who exclude from their presence the man whose sickness and suffering had separated him from the midst of the people of God. For in light of the resurrection of Jesus from the dead, the "other advocate," the Holy Spirit, makes something of the love between Jesus and the Father available to the community of God's people.[27] That availability makes possible a new politics—that is, a new way of living together—that includes a way of being with and caring for those whose sickness or suffering pulls them away from participation in the normal rhythms of life.

| | |

Divine Space and Time: Toward a Politics of Healing and Caring

The politics forming the foundation for a faithful Christian disposition toward sickness and suffering derives from God's self-revelation in the biblical stories of creation and redemption. One of the most significant things we learn as we stand back and observe the entire sweep of those stories is that the God revealed in them is revealed as a *society*: God is Father, Son, and Holy Spirit, not first one and then three, but at once one and three. "The being of God," explains John Zizioulas, "is a relational being."[28] Moreover, God's self-revelation as the triune society extends through time right up to the present; it is precisely in and through the concrete common life of that human community called church that God continues to reveal godself as the perfect society of the three divine persons.[29]

This suggests that, at least for the Christian, the fundamental modern opposition between the individual and the social is a theological mistake. The Christian does not exist as Christian prior to or apart from the society that is called church, and the proper life of the church is constitutive of, rather than a threat to, the Christian's pursuit of life's goods.[30] Within the constraints of a Christian account of human life, there is no blunt opposition between freedom and obligation. God is a perfect society constituted by the mutual love of the divine persons, and the Christian is afforded the possibility of participating in that love by learning, through the practices of her community, a concrete set of repeatable skills.[31] It is through the acquisition of these skills that the Christian learns that she is a creature, that she is "in a specific way bracketed by the life of the triune persons."[32] Learning to be a creature is thus one way of describing redemption.

Learning to name ourselves and to live as creatures suggests that we also (re)learn a corresponding truth, namely, that our existence is the gift of a Creator. It has long since been an axiom in the Christian tradition that the society constituted by the mutual love of Father, Son, and Holy Spirit is an *aseity*. God is sufficient in and unto godself, which means that the act of creation is gratuitous and is not the obligatory fulfillment of an abstract divine entelechy. Creation is an absolutely voluntary overflowing of God's plenteous love: "for God to create is for him to *make accommodation* in his triune life for other persons and things than the three whose mutual life he is. In himself, he *opens room*, and that act is the event of creation."[33]

What this suggests is that the divine acts of creation and redemption are acts by which the mutual love binding the persons of the godhead are generously extended as well to us. God makes within godself time and space for us: "God takes time in his time for us. That is his act of creation."[34] And this is one of the senses in which redeemed creation is called to bear God's image. To be a creature is to live in pursuit of a divinely ordained telos within a web of materially dense moral relationships.[35] Because God is social, so are we called to be social, to live our lives for God and for those others for whom God has made room.

If I am created by a word from beyond me, I must hearken to what is beyond me, and then I hear not only God but you. Or rather, . . . I hear you *in* hearing God: in the church I hear God's gospel from the mouth of his witnesses; and in the world I hear God's law from the mouth even of those of his counterparts who do not rightly identify him. If I pray, and pray with ritual embodiment, I just thereby become publicly available and so available to you, even should my prayer itself be misaddressed.[36]

We see here the beginnings of a pattern for a redeemed human society, and so for a hope-full set of practices of being sick among others and of caring for those others among us, especially those who are sick. A life oriented to God is a life of availability to those others who find their way into our lives. In creation and redemption, God makes and keeps time within godself for that which is other than God. Because God is social, otherness is not a threat to divine being; it is instead constitutive of that being. Similarly, the community that is the people of God is to be a community that as a matter of pure grace makes and maintains within itself time and space for often burdensome others.

Within such a community we may anticipate the display of certain characteristics. First, the society of God's people is at once radically exclusive and radically inclusive. It is an exclusive community because it determinatively abandons—that is, it *excludes*— the normative modern ideal of the self-interested individual woman or man. The community is inclusive, moreover, in that it creates and maintains space, pledging to be *with* and *for* all women and men without respect to the particular ways in which they may complicate the life of the community. Because the church is fundamentally a eucharistic community, it is a welcoming community, for the Eucharist is a celebration in anticipation of that great inclusive banquet celebrating God's perfect reign of peace and justice.[37]

This peculiar inclusive/exclusive character makes the Christian society at once purposefully insubordinate with respect to the dominant order ruled by the fallen powers and purposefully subordinate to the gospel mandate to be a servant to weakness. Because members of the Christian community do not aspire to or see themselves as acquisitive, self-interested individuals, the Christian understanding of normal human being includes the possibility of weakness and dependence and of the achievement of the human telos in and through weakness and dependence. Thus the Christian struggle against illness does not require in every instance that illness be eliminated in order for it to be resisted and defeated. The persistence of illness is not necessarily a sign that the Christian has conceded her struggle against it, for the way in which the Christian is ill in the presence of the community that gathers around and cares for her is itself a sign of the Kingdom, which is overcoming the brokenness of the fallen cosmos.[38] This is not to say that Christians experience illness as less painful or debilitating than non-Christians; illness is an awful, unpleasant, and serious business for all humans. Rather, the meaning of illness and the politics of the care of illness are transformed by its occurring within the Christian community. In the world of the acquisitive, self-interested individual, illness is a threat because it hinders the pursuit of individual goods. Sick people cannot work or enjoy the fruits of their work, and their sickness is typically understood as a burden to those (nonprofessionals) who care for them, a burden that keeps the caregivers from working or enjoying the fruits of *their* work. In the Christian community, illness poses an altogether different set of challenges.

Illness and caring for illness are thus always fundamentally political acts. For the Christian, the primary threat posed by illness is not that it threatens to destroy the body of the person, although that is certainly a legitimate concern that must be addressed, but that it alienates the ill member from those other members of the community on whom she is dependent for the achievement of life's greatest goods. The telos of the Christian life is not attainable apart from the mutual help and encouragement of friends, and friendship, as Aristotle reminds us, requires sharing time and proximity. A friend, according to Aristotle, is a "second self," someone who knows us as well as we know ourselves and in whose life we see reflected back to us what we are becoming.[39] To be a friend of the sick is not an easy thing—sick people, after all, are not much fun to be around—and to be a sick friend is probably even harder. This is why the friendship at the center of a good Christian disposition toward sickness and suffering requires the cultivation of certain virtues, and especially of the virtue Thomas Aquinas called *misericordia*, or mercy, which is that virtue by which we are moved to act for the benefit of another whom we see suffering.[40]

Misericordia derives from the foundational Christian virtue of charity, that perfect love of God that, according to Aquinas, "signifies not only love of God but also a certain friendship with God."[41] Misericordia, then, has to do first of all with friendship with God, then with human friendship, and finally with hospitality to the stranger.[42] From the perspective of misericordia it is not ultimately important whether the other to whose service we are moved to come is a friend, a family member, or a relative stranger, for to possess the virtue of misericordia, explains Alasdair MacIntyre, is to make of a stranger a kind of friend.[43] And this is an achievement requiring the development and exercise of the moral imagination. For it is only as we successfully and realistically imagine ourselves in the place of the other that we can be moved to act for their genuine good, as their "second self."

Aquinas calls this capacity "a defect in the person who pities,"[44] which seems a very strange way of characterizing a virtue. But if we read on, we discover exactly what it is that Aquinas means. Because misericordia, he says, is a kind of sorrow, and because sorrow only exists in the presence of some sort of defect—that is, something that causes pain or suffering—then misericordia can only exist in the presence of a defect. Now Aquinas anticipates the claim that the defect to which one responds in the exercise of misericordia is in the person who is suffering, rather than the person who is responding. He does this by arguing that the very fact that the distress of another can move us to action is evidence that we have imagined ourselves in their place. For "since sorrow or grief is about one's *own* ills, one grieves or sorrows for another's distress, in so far as one looks upon another's distress *as one's own*."[45] And one can look upon another's distress as one's own only as one can imagine oneself in the place of that other.

What might the exercise of the virtue of misericordia look like in the immediate context of the Christian community's care of the sick, and more important, what difference might its exercise make? These are questions we are not altogether sure how to answer, since there is a very real sense in which virtue, like any skill, is fully understood only when it is embodied and displayed. We can, on the other hand, offer some preliminary reflections that might deflect what we anticipate will be questions or concerns with the argument we have been developing here.

First of all, the exercise of misericordia by any one member of a community carries with it the possibility of transforming the entire community. A serious, thoughtful attempt to imagine oneself in a position of profound dependence, as unpleasant as that may be, will almost certainly reveal to us something Aquinas held as axiomatic. The virtues do not exist in their fullest sense apart from one another. In the particular case of misericordia, what this means is that there is an inextricable connectedness of giving mercy with receiving mercy.[46] Which is to say that we can be fully merciful only when we can imagine ourselves also as gracious receivers of mercy.

In such an act of imagination, we discover that one of the ways we frequently hear others and ourselves speak about the prospects of our own impending illness, decline, and death is fundamentally self-deceptive. The often-repeated phrase, "I don't want to be a burden" is largely a reflection of this society's cult of the self-sufficient, autonomous individual and thus a mask covering one of the most basic truths of our existence. We are all, at all times, burdening and being burdened. Indeed, we are probably never more human than when we are burdening another or bearing another's burdens. It is given to each of us at various times in our lives to bear the burdens of others in particular ways, according to our particular gifts, and at other times to allow our burdens to be borne.

Second, the exercise of misericordia carries with it the possibility of transforming the caregiver's world. As we place ourselves in the position of being second selves to the sick, and as we realize the extent to which disability and suffering are inherent in the human condition, we realize as well the extent to which friendship and misericordia are necessary constituents of the Christian society. For in the Christian society, as MacIntyre suggests, our regard for others is never "diminished or abolished by what happens to the other, by his or her afflictions."[47]

Such a society is finally possible only when we realize that—and act as if—the sick are of genuine value and that *even in the midst of their sufferings and disabilities* they make a genuine, substantive contribution to our common good. This will not happen because we come to an agreement about a set of formal criteria by which we can identify another as a person. Rather, it will happen because we collectively come to realize that our relationships to them are never simply one-sided. What the disabled entrusted to our care give us, explains McIntyre, is:

> the possibility of learning something essential, what it is for someone else to be wholly entrusted to our care, so that we are answerable for their well-being. Everyone of us has, as an infant, been wholly entrusted to someone else's care, so that they were answerable for our well-being. Now we have the opportunity to learn just what it is to owe such individuals by learning for ourselves what it is to be so entrusted.[48]

Being so entrusted means, as we have said, making the best possible use of our several gifts for the benefit of the other. But in the final analysis it cannot mean *only* this. For when we are made second selves to those who suffer, we are also committed to being among those who represent them and their interests to the wider political body.[49] And this will inevitably change that body. A political world in which the interests of the ill are *personally* represented will no longer be a world constituted only by the need to balance and adjudicate between competing individual self-interests. Nor will it be a world dominated by the alienating demands of market capitalism.[50] Rather, it will be a world in which the inherent interdependence of human being is acknowledge and appreciated, a world in which the interrelationship of our goods and the goods of those entrusted to our care become evident.

|||

Belonging and Being With

For a glimpse at such a world, we return in conclusion to Port William and the life shared by the membership there. In the story "Fidelity," Berry allows us to share in the last days of one of the membership's central characters, Burley Coulter. At the story's beginning we see Burley, who is in a hospital in the distant city of Louisville, through the minds' eyes of his son Danny and his daughter-in-law, Lyda, who at night lay sleepless, "disturbed beyond the power to think by the thought of the old man who was lying slack and still in the mechanical room, in the merciless light, with a tube in his nose and a tube needled into his arm and a tube draining his bladder into a plastic bag that hung beneath the bed."[51]

Clearly, Burley is dying. Yet it is not his death that keeps those who love him awake at night but the circumstances of his dying—the manner in which he is being made to die. He has been cut off from those with whom he has shared his life, for even though they are in his hospital room every night, there they are "offering themselves where they could not be received." Berry writes: "They were brought back as if by mere habit into the presence of a life that had once included them and now did not, for it was a life that, so far as they could see, no longer included even itself."[52]

What is compelling about the story "Fidelity" is its account of how Burley has come to be separated from those to whose life included his own and, more important, how he comes to be returned to them. Both his going and his coming back are the result of his friends' and family's love for him. When Burley became ill, the women and men who loved him took him, perhaps against their better judgment, to the doctor "because they wanted to do more for him than they could do, and they could think of nothing else."[53] Yet in spite of the best efforts of the physicians and nurses in Louisville, he continues to decline. When he lapses into a coma, his physicians remain stubbornly optimistic, convinced of his eventual recovery. Soon, however, his family sees that recovery is not likely.

When they returned on yet another visit and found the old body still as it had been, a mere passive addition to the complicated machines that kept it minimally alive, they saw finally that in their attempt to help they had not helped but only complicated his disease beyond their power to help. And they thought with regret of the time when the thing that was wrong with him had been simply unknown, and there had been only it and him and him and them in the place they had known together. Loving him, wanting to help him, they had given him over to "the best of modern medical care"—which meant, as they now saw, that they had abandoned him.[54]

The point here is not that medicine and medical technology are bad but that medicine and medical technology are *for* something. They exist not for their own sake but are at their best when they are in the service of, and contributing to, human flourishing. And human flourishing does not simply include but requires membership in a community of friends who love one another. When technology removes us from such communities, especially when there is little possibility that it will be able to return us to them, it is by definition no longer contributing to our flourishing. Some of the Port William membership, those who have been the closest members of the life that has been Burley Coulter, have made a mistake, and they respond to it now as those of us who know them have come to expect, by going back and making it right, by overcoming the wound that is the separation of the life of one of their own from their life together.

In the middle of the night, Danny goes to the hospital and takes Burley away, disconnecting the tubes joining him to the world of the hospital and removing him secretly to another world altogether in a place both men know and love. There, in an old barn in a long since overgrown hollow, Danny stays with the old man, talking to him, comforting him, and reassuring him as he slips away into death, "You're all right. You don't have to worry about a thing."[55] Carefully, Danny digs a grave beneath a tree in the hollow, reminding himself all the time, "These are the last things now. Everything that happens now happens for the last time in his life."[56] And finally, when Burley has taken his last breath, Danny buries him, speaking aloud the simple prayer, "Be with him, as he has been with us."[57] When asked later to account for his actions, Danny says only "I had an account to settle with one of my creditors."[58]

This, finally, is at the center of what it means to be sick as a Christian, to suffer as a Christian, or to be present as a Christian to those who are sick or suffering. It is to know that life—being, if you will—is a matter of being-with. It is to know that we belong, in sickness and in health, in flourishing and in suffering, to God and to one another. It is to know that our stewardship of each other's lives makes every one of us debtors to every other one, because in every aspect of our lives and then in our deaths, we belong to God and to one another. It means that we must take time and to make room, understanding that being sick and especially being with those who are sick or suffering does not take time away from life. Rather, these are the things of life itself.

Notes

Introduction

1 See Marilynne Robinson, *The Death of Adam: Essays on Modern Thought* (Boston: Houghton Mifflin, 1998), p. 80.

2 Romans 8:18–23, NRSV.

3 See, for example, Dale Matthews, David Larson, and Constance Berry, *The Faith Factor: An Annotated Bibliography of Clinical Research on Spiritual Subjects* (Rockville, MD: National Institute for Healthcare Research, 1993). This two-volume bibliography covers some four hundred pages and contains the abstracts from more than 150 studies.

4 For a good characterization of these studies and the struggle to interpret their results, see two articles by Jeffrey Levin: "Religion and Health: Is There an Association, Is It Valid, and Is It Causal?" *Social Science and Medicine* 38(11), 1994, pp. 1475–1482, and "How Religion Influences Morbidity and Health: Reflections on Natural History, Salutogenesis and Host Resistance," *Social Science and Medicine* 43(5), 1996, pp. 849–864.

5 Consider the following: Herbert Benson, *Beyond the Relaxation Response* (New York: Berkley Books, 1985), and *Timeless Healing* (New York: Scribner, 1996); Larry Dossey, *Prayer Is Good Medicine* (San Francisco: Harper, 1996), and *Reinventing Medicine* (San Francisco: Harper, 1999); Harold Koenig, *The Healing Power of Faith* (New York: Simon and Schuster, 1999), and *Is Religion Good for Your Health?* (New York: Haworth Pastoral Press, 1997); Dale Matthews, *The Faith Factor: Proof of the Healing Power of Prayer* (New York: Penguin, 1998).

6 In all fairness, most of the authors with whom we contend in this book do not write with an explicit concern for Christian faithfulness. Nor, however, as many of them insist, do they write from the perspective of a theologically neutral "religion" that can be applied unproblematically to any person regardless of his or her particular beliefs.

7 Basil, "The Long Rules," in *Saint Basil: Ascetical Works*, Monica Wagner, trans. (Washington, DC: Catholic University of America Press, 1962), p. 331. Quoted in H. Tristam Engelhardt, "Genetic Enhancement and Theosis: Two Models of Therapy," in *Christian Bioethics* 5(2), 1999, p. 198.

8 Harold Bloom, *The American Religion: The Emergence of the Post-Christian Nation* (New York: Simon and Schuster, 1992), p. 37.

9 Ibid, p. 32.

10 Rowan Williams, *Lost Icons: Reflections on Cultural Bereavement* (Edinburgh: T & T Clark, 2000), p. 23.

11 As we were preparing this introduction, a friend called our attention to an article published by the Reuters news service entitled "'The Pope Meets Aerosmith in MAXX's 'Spiritual Market.'" The subject of the article is a recently established company that offers "products and services that fulfill spiritual longings that transcend the lines of organized religion." According to the company's founder, the aim is "to capture the spiritual marketplace." It is especially interesting to note that this article appeared online on the finance page of the website individual.com, which is devoted to helping small businesses market their products. For an interesting critical account of the ways this religious consumerism is present in contemporary American Christianity, see Phil Kenneson and James Street, *Selling Out the Church* (Nashville: Abingdon Press, 1997).

12 See, for example, the July-August 1998 issue of the *Utne Reader*, entitled "Designer God." The article "God With a Million Faces," by Jeremiah Creedon (pp. 42–48), is an especially interesting discussion of contemporary religiosity.

13 Bloom, p. 27.

14 Here see K. G. Meador and S. C. Henson, "Growing Old in a Therapeutic Culture," *Theology Today* 57(2), 2000, pp. 185–202.

15 For helpful discussions of ideology and knowledge, see Denys Turner, *Marxism and Christianity* (Totowa, NJ: Barnes and Noble, 1983), pp. 1–81, and Nicholas Lash, *A Matter of Hope* (Notre Dame, IN: University of Notre Dame Press, 1982), pp. 125–134.

16 For a good review of the development of the way we have been shaped by modernity to understand the relationship between science and human limitations—especially limitations of the body—see Gerald McKenny, *To Relieve the Human Condition* (Albany: State University of New York Press, 1997), pp. 7–75. See also Joel Shuman, "Desperately Seeking Perfection: Christian Discipleship and Medical Genetics," in *Christian Bioethics* 5(2), 2000, pp. 139–153.

17 Daniel Callahan, "Death and the Research Imperative," in *The New England Journal of Medicine*, 342 (9), 2000, p. 654.

18 For a very clear account of how this understanding shapes and problematizes the ways we care for one another, see Charles Taylor, "Philosophical Reflections on Caring Practices" in *The Crisis of Care*, edited by Susan Phillips and Patricia Benner. (Washington, DC: Georgetown University Press, 1994), pp. 175–187.

19 Wendell Berry, "Health as Membership," in *Another Turn of the Crank* (Washington, DC: Counterpoint, 1995), p. 89. See. Joel Shuman, *The Body of Compassion* (Boulder, CO: Westview Press, 1999).

20 Christopher Lasch, *The True and Only Heaven* (New York: Norton, 1991), p. 518.

21 Dan Beauchamp has written persuasively about the "market prison" in which contemporary medicine finds itself incarcerated in *The Health of the Republic* (Philadelphia: Temple University Press, 1988).

22 More than in any other developed country, medicine developed in the United States as a variety of small business. See David Rothman, "A Century of Failure: Class Barriers to Reform" in *The Politics of Health Care Reform*, edited by James Morone and Gary Belkin (Durham, NC: Duke University Press, 1994), pp. 11–25.

23 Stephen Crook, Jan Pakulski, and Malcolm Waters, *Postmodernization: Change in Advanced Society* (London: Sage, 1992), pp. 58–61. The authors argue persuasively that the concept of "lifestyle" as a way of life chosen by the individual is the product of the hypercommodification characteristic of late modernity.

24 John Kavanaugh, *Following Christ in a Consumer Society*, 2nd ed. (Maryknoll, NY: Orbis, 1991), p. 31.

25 Berry, p. 86.

26 Ibid., p. at 90.

27 Augustine, *Confessions*, 1. 1 (1).

28 Ibid., 4. 4.9.

29 Augustine, *The Catholic and Munichaean Ways of Life*, 1.3(4); 1.20(37). See Donald Burt, *Friendship and Society* (Grand Rapids, MI: Eerdmans, 1999), p. 5.

30 Burt, p. 45.

31 Augustine, *On Christian Doctrine*, 1.3.3.

32 Ibid., 1.4.4.

33 See *Confessions*, 10.37.61; See Burt, p. 45.

34 Nicholas Lash, *The Beginning and the End of "Religion"* (Notre Dame, IN: University of Notre Dame Press, 1996), p. 21.

35 Ibid., p. 35.

36 Ibid., p. 37.

37 Ibid.

38 On this point, see Paul Waddell, *Friendship and the Moral Life* (Notre Dame, IN: University of Notre Dame Press, 1989), Alasdair MacIntyre, *Three Rival Versions of Moral Enquiry* (Notre Dame, IN: University of Notre Dame Press, 1990), and L. Gregory Jones, *Transformed Judgment* (Notre Dame, IN: University of Notre Dame Press, 1990).

39 Michael Buckley, *At the Origins of Modern Atheism* (New Haven: Yale University Press, 1987), p. 31.

40 John Howard Yoder, *The Politics of Jesus* (Grand Rapids, MI: Eerdmans, 1972), p. 238.

41 Guenter B. Risse, *Mending Bodies, Saving Souls: A History of Hospitals* (New York: Oxford University Press, 1999).

42 Karl Barth, *The Humanity of God* (Louisville: John Knox Press, 1960), p. 62.

Chapter 1

1 For an especially interesting analysis of this trend, see Marilynne Robinson's essay "Facing Reality," in *The Death of Adam: Essays on Modern Thought* (Boston: Houghton Mifflin, 1998), pp. 76–85. See also Michael Walzer, *Spheres of Justice* (New York: Basic Books, 1983), p. 87.

2 Daniel Callahan, "Death and the Research Imperative," *The New England Journal of Medicine*, 342(9), 2000, p. 654.

3 Wendell Berry, "Health as Membership," in *Another Turn of the Crank* (Washington, DC: Counterpoint, 1995), pp. 86–109.

4 A recent computer search of a popular medical database for articles on "religion and medicine" yielded more than four thousand items, more than two hundred of which were published after 1999.

5 For a representative review of the literature supporting this broad claim, see: C. G. Ellison and J. S. Levin, "The Religion-Health Connection: Evidence, Theory, and Future Directions," *Health Education and Behavior* 25(6), 1998, pp. 700–720.

6 We will for the present hold in abeyance the question of whether there is more than a family resemblance between such traditions and whether the generic term "religion" has more than heuristic meaning. As Christians, we are reticent to speak—even a little—for any other tradition. For the present, we will use words like "religion," "religious faith," and "religious practices" to refer to the way those notions function within particular religious traditions, as well as for the rather more casual way they are used to refer to individual beliefs divorced from concrete traditions. This question is significant for the argument we wish to make in this book, and we discuss it in some detail in chapter 2.

7 Nicholas Lash, *The Beginning and the End of "Religion"* (Notre Dame, IN: University of Notre Dame Press, 1996), pp. 19–22.

8 Roy Porter, "Religion and Medicine," in *The Companion Encyclopedia of the History of Medicine*, vol. 2, edited by W. F. Bynum and Roy Porter, p. 1449; see Robert Sevensky, "The Religious Foundations of Health Care: A Conceptual Approach," *Journal of Medical Ethics*, 9(3), 1983, p. 165.

9 Porter, pp. 1449, 1456.

10 Sevensky, p. 166.

11 Gert Brieger, "The Historiography of Medicine," in Bynum and Porter, *Companion Encyclopedia*, pp. 24–44, suggests that until recently, many histories of medicine have expressed a largely positivist view. For examples of histories of medicine of this sort, see: Howard Haggard, *Mystery, Magic and Medicine: The Rise of Medicine from Superstition to Science* (Garden City, NJ: Doubleday and Doran, 1933); Lester King, *The Growth of Medical Thought* (Chicago: University of Chicago Press, 1963); Henry Sigerist, *The Great Doctors* (Garden City, NJ: Doubleday, 1958); and, more recently, Sherwin Nulland, *Doctors: The Biography of Medicine* (New York: Vintage, 1988).

12 Ibid., p. 165.

13 Porter (p. 1462) notes: "The triumph of the mechanical philosophy through Descartes (1596–1650), Newton (1642–1727), and their followers . . . buttressed iatromechanistic models of medicine, viewing the body as a machine, and thus putting a practical medicine/religion dualism upon a new footing." For a summary of some of the less happy effects of medicine's wholesale adoption of the iatromechanical model, see Joel Shuman, *The Body of Compassion* (Boulder, CO: Westview Press, 1999), pp. 10–16, 22–28.

14 See Ivan Illich, *Medical Nemesis: The Expropriation of Health* (New York: Pantheon, 1976), p. 30.

15 Larry Dossey, *Reinventing Medicine* (San Francisco: HarperCollins, 1999), pp. 13–36.

16 David Browder, "Elected Suffering: Toward a Theology for Medicine," Ph.D. diss., at Duke University, 1991, p. 30. Browder shows very nicely the influence of Comtean positivism on an emergent scientific medicine in the nineteenth century and the ongoing influence of positivism in contemporary medicine.

17 Christopher Ellison and Jeffrey Levin, "The Religion-Health Connection: Evidence, Theory, and Future Directions," *Health Education and Behavior* 25(6), December 1998, p. 701. See Jeffrey Levin, "Religion and Health: Is There an Association, Is It Valid, and Is It Causal?" *Social Science and Medicine* 38(11), 1994, p. 1475, and "How Religion Influences Morbidity and Health: Reflections on Natural History, Salutogenesis and Host Resistance," *Social Science and Medicine* 43(5), 1996, p. 849.

18 Ellison and Levin, p. 701.

19 Levin, "Religion and Health," p. 1476; see Dale Matthews et al., "Religious Commitment and Health Status," *Archives of Family Medicine* 8(6), 1999, p. 476.

20 Dale Matthews, Dale Larson, and Constance Berry, *The Faith Factor: An Annotated Bibliography of Clinical Research on Spiritual Subjects*, vol. 1 (Rockville, MD: National Institute for Healthcare Research, 1993), pp. 11, 25, 87, 95–96, 121, 123, 126, 177–178.

21 Jeffrey Dwyer et al., "The Effects of Religious Concentration and Affiliation on County Cancer Mortality Rates," *Journal of Health and Social Behavior* 31, 1990, p. 189.

22 Ibid., p. 195.

23 Harold Koenig et al., "Attendance at Religious Services, Interleukin-6, and Other Biological Parameters of Immune Function in Older Adults," *International Journal of Psychiatry in Medicine* 27(3), 1997, pp. 233–250.

24 Harold Koenig et al., "The Relationship between Religious Activities and Blood Pressure in Older Adults," *International Journal of Psychiatry in Medicine* 28(2), 1998, pp. 189–213.

25 Harold Koenig and David Larson, "Use of Hospital Services, Religious Attendance, and Religious Affiliation," *Southern Medical Journal* 91(10), 1998, pp. 925–932.

26 Ellison and Levin, pp. 702–703. The authors point out that a new generation

of more rigorous studies for the most part confirm what the earlier studies suggested: there is a positive link between religion and health.

27 R. P. Sloan et al., "Religion, Spirituality and Medicine," *Lancet* 353, 1999, pp. 664–667. More recently, see the editorial by R. P. Sloan et al., *The New England Journal of Medicine* 342(25), 2000, pp. 1913–1916.

28 Ibid., p. 665–666.

29 Ibid., p. 666. Indeed, from a more distinctly theological point of view, this is our most significant argument with the faith and health movement.

30 Larry Dossey, "Do Religion and Spirituality Matter in Health? A Response to the Recent Article in *The Lancet*," *Alternative Therapies* 5(3), 1999, pp. 16–18, and Harold Koenig et al., "Religion, Spirituality, and Medicine: A Rebuttal to Skeptics," *International Journal of Psychiatry in Medicine* 29(2), 1999, pp. 123–131, both respond to Sloan's concerns. They make strong counterarguments defending the quality and significance of the research done to this point. But in addressing Sloan's conceptual and ethical concerns, they do little more than take the other side in an intractable and by now quite tired discussion in contemporary mainstream bioethics, namely the blunt juxtaposition of patient autonomy with physician authority.

31 Ellison and Levin, pp. 702–703.

32 Levin, "Religion and Health," p. 1477.

33 Ibid., p. 1480.

34 Levin ("Religion and Health," pp. 1478–1480), for example, suggests several "alternative hypotheses" explaining the association, including behavior, heredity, psychosocial effects, and so forth.

35 This is one of the weaknesses of the critique by Sloan et al., who presume in "Religion, Spirituality, and Medicine" that "religion" is something other than the social practices that typically accompany it. The point is dealt with quite nicely by Koenig et al., "Religion, Spirituality and Medicine," pp. 125–126.

36 Levin, "Religion and Health," pp. 1477–1478.

37 Levin, "How Religion Influences," pp. 854–856.

38 We defend this claim in some detail in chapters 2 and 3. For an account of the phenomenon of consumerism in medicine, see Marie Haug and Bebe Levin, *Consumerism in Medicine* (Beverly Hills, CA: Sage, 1983).

39 See, for example, Arthur Kleinman, *The Illness Narratives* (New York: Basic Books, 1981); Arthur Frank, *At the Will of the Body* (Boston: Houghton Mifflin, 1991); Alasdair MacIntyre, "Patients as Agents," in *Philosophical Medical Ethics: Its Nature and Significance*, edited by S. F. Spicker and H. T. Engelhardt (Dordrecht: D. Reidel, 1977).

40 We will not argue this point here; for a very good argument against dualism, see Berry, "Health as Membership," pp. 86–109.

41 Ibid., pp. 93–96.

42 Ibid., p. 87.

43 Edmund Pellegrino and David Thomasma, *A Philosophical Basis of Medical Practice* (New York: Oxford University Press, 1981), p. 17.

44 Ibid., pp. 71, 47.

45 Alasdair MacIntyre, "Medicine Aimed at the Care of Persons Rather Than What . . . ?" in Spicker and Engelhardt, *Philosophical Medical Ethics*, pp. 83–103.

46 Ibid., pp. 73–75, 106–108.

47 See Berry, "Health as Membership."

48 Ibid., p. 125.

49 Ibid., pp. 126–135.

50 On the matters of narrative, practices, and social relations, see Alasdair Mac-Intyre, *After Virtue*, 2nd ed. (Notre Dame, IN: University of Notre Dame Press, 1984).

51 D. E. King and B. Bushwick, "Beliefs and Attitudes of Hospital Inpatients about Faith Healing and Prayer," *Journal of Family Practice* 39(4), 1994, pp. 349–352; Bernard Lo et al., "Discussing Palliative Care with Patients," *Annals of Internal Medicine* 130(9), 1999, pp. 744–749.

52 Marion Danis et al., "Incorporating Palliative Care into Critical Care Education: Principles, Challenges, and Opportunities," *Critical Care Medicine* 27(9), 1999, pp. 2005–2013.

53 Dale Matthews et al., "Religious Commitment and Health Status: A Review of the Research and Implications for Family Medicine," *Archives of Family Medicine* 7(2), 1998, pp. 118–124.

54 Ibid., p. 123.

55 Pellegrino and Thomasma, p. 88.

56 Ibid., p. 135.

57 Pellegrino and Thomasma offer a very good account of the philosophical history and the clinical application of the notion of judgment in their book, pp. 119–152.

58 Even Sloan et al. ("Religion, Spirituality, and Medicine") concede this point.

59 Lash, *The Beginning and the End of "Religion"*, p. 21.

60 For an account of the way the notion of "religion" tends to function in contemporary North American and European cultures, see the article by Ingolf Dalferth, "'I Determine What God Is!': Theology in the Age of 'Cafeteria Religion,'" *Theology Today* 57(1), 2000, pp. 5–23.

61 See, for example, Harold Koenig, *The Healing Power of Faith* (New York: Simon and Schuster, 1999), pp. 22–23.

62 Ibid., p. 26.

63 Ibid., pp. 26–27.

64 Herbert Benson, *Beyond the Relaxation Response* (New York: Berkley, 1984), p. 5.

65 Ibid., p. 8, emphasis in original.

66 Ibid., pp. 81–82.

67 On this point, see Benson, *Beyond the Relaxation Response*, p. 6, and Koenig, *Healing Power of Faith*, p. 23.

68 Benson, *Relaxation Response*, pp. 24–25.

69 Herbert Benson, *Timeless Healing* (New York: Scribner, 1996), p. 200.

70 Larry Dossey, *Prayer Is Good Medicine* (San Francisco: Harper, 1996), p. xiii.

71 Ibid., p. xiv.

72 Quoted in Larry Dossey, *Healing Words* (San Francisco: Harper, 1993), p. xiii.

73 Dossey, *Prayer Is Good Medicine*, pp. 44–45.

74 Ibid., pp. 16–17.

75 Dossey, *Healing Words*, p. 7.

76 The exception here is Dossey, who is characteristically more careful. He begins his *Healing Words* with a fascinating catalogue of great spiritual masters who died untimely and often painful deaths, concluding that "the meaning of a particular disease may be *cosmic*—that is, it may be opaque and hidden to us mortals, known only to the Divine. On balance, this case warns us against equating spiritual and physical health, and cautions us against attributing shallow, superficial meaning to illness" (p. 15). Prayer can always, he says, elicit a cure, but: "By 'cure' I do not mean the *physical* disappearance of cancer, heart disease, high blood pressure, or stroke, but something more marvelous—the realization that *physical illness, no matter how painful or grotesque, is at some level of secondary importance in the total scheme of our existence*" (pp. 35–36, emphasis in original). Insofar as this represents Dossey's thinking on faith and health, his position bears certain strong resemblances to our own. It is not clear to us, however, how representative of his position this passage is, given the extent to which his book addresses the physical effects of prayer.

77 Herbert Benson, "The Nocebo Effect: History and Physiology," in *Preventive Medicine* 26, 1997, p. 612.

78 Ibid., p. 614.

79 For a thoughtful consideration of these matters, see Ellison and Levin, pp. 712–714.

80 Richard Wentz, "The Domestication of the Divine," *Theology Today* 57(1), 2000, p. 25.

81 Benson, *Timeless Healing*, p. 191.

82 Ibid., p. 299.

83 Ibid., p. 300.

84 Koenig, *Healing Power of Faith*, p. 25.

85 Ibid., p. 26; see pp. 277–282.

86 George Lindbeck, *The Nature of Doctrine* (Philadelphia: Westminster Press, 1984), p. 16.

87 Ibid., p. 17.

88 Ibid., p. 22.

89 Ibid., p. 31.

90 Ibid., p. 31.

91 Ibid., p. 22.

92 Ibid., p. 18.

93 Ibid., p. 32.

94 Ibid., p. 33.

95 Ibid., p. 34.

96 Ibid., pp. 37–38.

97 Koenig, *Healing Power of Faith*, p. 277; emphasis in original.

98 In chapters 2 and 3 we offer a more detailed account of the origins and content of this religion.

99 Harold Bloom, *The American Religion: The Emergence of the Post-Christian Nation* (New York: Simon and Schuster, 1992), p. 27.

100 Robert Jenson, "How the World Lost Its Story," *First Things*, October 1993, pp. 19–24.

101 Hans Frei, *The Eclipse of Biblical Narrative* (New Haven: Yale University Press, 1974).

102 Lash, *The Beginning and the End of "Religion,"* p. 148.

103 See Michel Foucault, *Power/Knowledge*, edited by Colin Gordon, translated by Coin Gordon et al. (New York: Pantheon, 1980); *The History of Sexuality*, vol. 1, *An Introduction,* translated by Robert Hurley (New York: Random House, 1978); *Discipline and Punish* (New York: Vintage, 1979); *Michel Foucault: Beyond Structuralism and Hermeneutics,* edited by Herbert Dreyfus and Paul Rabinow (Chicago: University of Chicago Press, 1982); and Alasdair MacIntyre, *After Virtue,* 2nd edition (Notre Dame, IN: University of Notre Dame Press, 1984).

104 Robert Jenson, *Systematic Theology*, vol. 2, *The Works of God* (New York: Oxford University Press, 1999), p. 315, emphasis added.

105 Jenson, "How the World Lost Its Story."

106 Michael Novak, *The Spirit of Democratic Capitalism* (London: IEA Health and Welfare Unit, 1991), pp. 341, 285. Quoted in Lash, *The Beginning and the End of "Religion,"* p. 187.

107 Lash, *The Beginning and the End of "Religion,"* p. 21.

108 Jenson, *Systematic Theology,* vol. 2, *The Works of God*, p. 318.

109 Gary Dorrien, *Soul in Society: The Making and Remaking of Social Christianity* (Minneapolis: Fortress Press, 1995), p. 339.

110 Ibid., p. 216.

111 Jenson, "How the World Lost Its Story."

112 Ibid.

Chapter 2

1 The endorsements by clergy on the covers and dust jackets of the popular books are telling in this regard. Consider, for example, that Koenig's *Healing Power of Faith* is endorsed by the Crystal Cathedral's Robert Schuller, the Southern Baptist Convention's Paige Patterson, and Elizabeth Peale Allen, daughter of the late Norman Vincent Peale.

2 Ingolf Dalferth, "'I Determine What God Is!': Theology in an Age of 'Cafeteria Religion,'" *Theology Today*, 57(1), April 2000, pp. 5–23.

3 John Rawls, *Political Liberalism* (New York: Columbia University Press, 1993), p. xxvi.

4 Dalferth, p. 7.

5 John Milbank, *Theology and Social Theory: Beyond Secular Reason* (Cambridge, MA: Blackwell, 1990), p. 1.

6 Nicholas Lash, *The Beginning and the End of "Religion"* (New York: Cambridge University Press, 1996), p. 11.

7 Rawls, p. xxv.

8 This perspective is one we have learned not only from Hume, who wrote a famous treatise, "On Miracles," about the impossibility of miracles, but also from nineteenth and twentieth-century liberal Protestant theologians like Ernst Troeltsch and the several inheritors of his legacy, from Rudolf Bultmann to H. Richard Niebuhr to James Gustafson.

9 Lash, p. 79.

10 John Milbank, "The Conflict of the Faculties: Theology and the Economy of the Sciences," unpublished paper, p. 20.

11 Lash, p. 79.

12 Ibid., pp. 12–13.

13 Ibid., p. 14.

14 Michel Foucault, *The Order of Things: An Archaeology of the Human Sciences* (New York: Vintage Books, 1973), p. xxii, emphasis in original.

15 Ibid., p. 17.

16 Ibid., p. 29.

17 Lash, pp. 126, 169.

18 Ibid., p. 12.

19 Richard Wentz, "The Domestication of the Divine," *Theology Today* 57(1), April 2000, pp. 24–34.

20 According to Lindbeck: "Three regulative principles at least were at work. First, there is the monotheistic principle: there is only one God, the God of Abraham, Isaac, Jacob, and Jesus. Second, there is the principle of historical specificity: the stories of Jesus refer to a genuine human being who was born, lived and died in a particular time and place. Third, there is the principle of what may be infelicitously called Christological maximalism: every possible importance is to be ascribed to Jesus that is not inconsistent with the first rules." *The Nature of Doctrine* (Philadelphia: Westminster Press, 1984), p. 94. See Lash, p. 133.

21 Lash, p. 19. See Alasdair MacIntyre, *After Virtue*, 2nd ed. (Notre Dame, IN: University of Notre Dame Press, 1984).

22 Michael Buckley, *At the Origins of Modern Atheism* (New Haven: Yale University Press, 1987), pp. 43, 48, 55. In what follows we depend heavily on Buckley's account of the development of religious thought in Europe from the seventeenth to nineteenth centuries. For a more nuanced account of how Thomas has been misread, see also Alasdair MacIntyre, *Three Rival Versions*

of *Moral Inquiry* (Notre Dame, IN: University of Notre Dame Press, 1990), pp. 58–81.

23 Buckley, p. 44.

24 Ibid., p. 47. Buckley notes: "While Lessius collapses in principle the distinction between metaphysics and ethics, he insists methodologically upon that between faith and reason, the distinction between 'credi et revelatione,' and 'multis rationibus, ex iis quae nobis nota sunt, et sensibus percipiuntur, solide probari posse.' They are separate areas of issues and methodology. Revelation is mentioned, connected with faith, and dismissed from consideration. Reasonings are mentioned, they are connected with proof or demonstration, and fifteen different 'rationes' are elaborated by which the truth of providence can be established." Whether Lessius's work is based in a *mis*reading of Aquinas is a matter of some dispute; compare Buckley, pp. 55, 341–343, to Lash, pp. 140–149. Buckley (p. 341) claims that the *"rationes* of Lessius owed more to the *De natura deorum* of Cicero than to any particular medieval theologian, but Lessius took from the Thomistic tradition an abrogation, the persuasion that the existence of god was essentially a philosophical problem rather than a theological or religious one." Lash, in our estimation, shows that this is a problematic reading of Thomas. This judgment is confirmed by Eugene Rogers's outstanding interpretation of Thomas in *Thomas Aquinas and Karl Barth: Sacred Doctrine and the Natural Knowledge of God* (Notre Dame, IN: University of Notre Dame Press, 1995).

25 Buckley, p. 52.

26 Ibid., p. 55.

27 This is not to say that Newton's was the only attempt to establish the existence of God by the application of scientific knowledge. As Buckley (pp. 68–92) points out, René Descartes had a similar interest, but because he was a mathematician, not a physicist, came to his conclusions in a very different way. Descartes's method, which began with and was based in radical doubt, grounded God's existence in the working of the free, immaterial mind—that is, in the mind that holds the *idea* of God—rather than in the working of the natural world. In grounding reality in the *cogito*, however, and positing a material reality that was absolutely passive, Descartes has posited a material reality from which traces of God's existence were absent. As we will soon show, these two approaches frequently come into contact with one another in the generations following Newton.

28 Buckley, p. 99.

29 Ibid., p. 102; see pp. 107–110.

30 Ibid., p. 120.

31 Ibid., p. 129.

32 Ibid., p. 131, emphasis added.

33 Ibid., p. 131.

34 Ibid., p. 132.

35 Ibid., pp. 135–138.

36 Ibid., p. 199.

37 Ibid., p. 200.

38 Ibid., p. 202.

39 Ibid., p. 203.

40 Ibid., p. 205.

41 Ibid., p. 211.

42 Ibid., p. 219.

43 Ibid., p. 219.

44 Ibid., p. 220.

45 Ibid.

46 Buckley notes (p. 254): "It is astonishing to see that [as, in the period following Diderot and Saunderson, materialism rose to ascendancy among European intellecuals] theology itself remains silent on this subject. One continues to accept the area of evidence that has been there since Lessius and has been developed by mechanists. The existence of God hangs from a theory of motion and matter."

47 See ibid., pp. 251–321.

48 Lash, pp. 16, 188.

49 Ibid., p. 189.

50 A. C. Ewing, *A Short Commentary on Kant's Critique of Pure Reason* (Chicago: University of Chicago Press, 1938), p. 16.

51 Ibid., pp. 11–12.

52 Buckley, p. 327. Ewing (p. 12) explains that Kant believed in a "'critical' philosophy, which will show that the categories can be proved, but only for the kind of objects which we encounter in science and ordinary experience."

53 Buckley, p. 328.

54 Immanuel Kant, *Religion Within the Limits of Reason Alone,* translated by Theodore Greene and Hoyt Hudson (New York: Harper and Row, 1960), p. 99.

55 Karl Barth, "Evangelical Theology in the Nineteenth Century," in *The Humanity of God* (Louisville: John Knox Press, 1960), p. 21. Barth's reference to a "sense and taste for the infinite" is taken from Schleiermacher.

56 Frederick Copleston, *A History of Philosophy*, vol 7 (New York: Doubleday, 1965), pp. 149–151.

57 Barth, "Evangelical Theology in the Ninettenth Century," p. 12.

58 Copleston, pp. 149, 152–153; see Buckley, p. 330.

59 Friedrich Schleiermacher, *On Religion: Speeches to Its Cultured Despisers,* translated by John Oman (New York: Harper, 1958) pp. 26–27. Schleiermacher offers a significant insight into his broad commitment to philosophical idealism here, when he says: "Nothing that is essentially characteristic and peculiar can be quite the same as that which openly exhibits and represents it."

60 Ibid., p. 27.

61 Ibid., p. 27.

62 Ibid., p. 33.

63 Ibid., p. 35.

64 Ibid., p. 36.

65 Ibid., p. 39.

66 Ibid., p. 39.

67 Ibid., p. 43.

68 Ibid., p. 45.

69 Ibid., p. 45. "Your feeling is piety, in so far as it expresses, in the manner described, the being and life common to you and to the All. Your feeling is piety in so far as it is the result of the operation of God in you by means of the operation of the world upon you."

70 Ibid,, p. 46.

71 Ibid., p. 48; see pp. 90–92.

72 Ibid., pp. 49–50.

73 Ibid., p. 50; see pp. 93–95.

74 Ibid., pp. 50–51.

75 Schleiermacher says (p. 87) that "dogmas and doctrines . . . are the result of that contemplation of feeling, of that reflection and comparison, of which we have already spoken. The conceptions that underlie these propositions are, like your conceptions from experience, nothing but general expressions for definite feelings. They are not necessary to religion itself, scarcely even for communicating religion, but reflection requires and creates them."

76 Ibid., p. 86. He goes on to say (p. 87), in what we take to be his application of the classical Christian doctrine of the Fall, not simply to humanity generally, but especially to his audience of "cultured despisers": "This result of human imperfection causes religion to appear dismembered. Religion takes the form of some peculiar receptivity and taste for art, philosophy or morality, and is consequently often mistaken."

77 Ibid., p. 101.

78 Ibid.

79 Friedrich Schleiermacher, *The Christian Faith*, English translation of the 2nd German edition, edited by H. Mackintosh and J. Stewart (Edinburgh: T. and T. Clark, 1989), p. 13.

80 Ibid., p. 14.

81 Ibid., p. 15.

82 Ibid., p. 15.

83 Ibid., p. 20.

84 Ibid., p. 15.

85 Ibid., p. 21.

86 Ibid., p. 12; see *Speeches*, pp. 105–106.

87 Ibid., p. 27; emphasis in original.

88 Ibid., p. 28.

89 Ibid., p. 31.

90 Karl Barth, *Church Dogmatics* vol. 1, pt. 1, edited by G. W. Bromley and T. F. Torrance (Edinburgh: T. and T. Clark, 1975), p. 211.

91 Alasdair MacIntyre, *Marxism and Christianity* (Notre Dame, IN: University of Notre Dame Press, 1984), p. 7.

92 Ibid., p. 11.

93 Ibid., pp. 7–8.

94 Ibid., p. 12.

95 Ibid., p. 13.

96 Van Harvey, *Feuerbach and the Interpretation of Religion* (Cambridge, England: Cambridge University Press, 1995), p. 72.

97 Ibid., p. 72.

98 Ibid., pp. 25–39.

99 Ludwig Feuerbach, *Lectures on the Essence of Religion* (hereafter *LER*), translated by Ralph Manheim (New York: Harper and Row, 1967), p. 17. He goes on in this passage to say: "in other words, the object of religion, which in Greek we call *theos* and in our language God, expresses nothing other than the essence of man; man's God is nothing other than the deified essence of man, so that the history of religion or, what amounts to the same thing, of God—for the gods are as varied as the religions, and the religions are as varied as mankind—is nothing other than the history of man."

100 *LER*, p. 67. Quoted in Harvey, p. 177.

101 Milbank, *Theology and Social Theory*, p. 180.

102 Ibid.

103 Ludwig Feuerbach, *The Essence of Christianity* (hereafter *EC*), translated by George Eliot (New York: Harper, 1957), p. 1.

104 Ibid., p. 2.

105 Ibid., p. 3.

106 Ibid., p. 8.

107 See Harvey, p. 40. Of course, there remains a significant difference between the two; Schleiermacher was never so bold as to claim, as did Feuerbach, that just to the extent humans are self-conscious they are not only religious, but also divine.

108 *EC*, p. 23.

109 Ibid., p. 26.

110 Ibid., pp. 29–30.

111 *LER*, p. 199.

112 Ibid., p. 25.

113 This is not to say that Feuerbach thought the abandonment of paganism represented a turn from utility; it simply became more complex. He remarks (*LER*, p. 200): "In short, religion has essentially a practical aim and foundation; the drive that gives rise to religion, its ultimate foundation, is the striving for happiness, and if this is an egoistic drive, it follows that the ultimate foundation of religion is egoism . . . at the lowest and at the highest levels."

114 Ibid., pp. 58–62.

115 *EC*, p. 122, emphasis in original.

116 *LER*, p. 237.

117 Ibid., pp. 203–204.

118 Van Harvey (p. 176) makes the important point that Feuerbach's use of the term "egoism" is not to be understood pejoratively. Feuerbach simply believed that the universal human feeling of dependence was an expression of the fact that when all is said and done, each person is defined inescapably by his or her individual desires.

119 *EC*, p. 123.

120 Harvey, p. 23; see p. 176.

121 *EC*, p. 135.

Chapter 3

1 Van Harvey, *Feuerbach and the Interpretation of Religion* (Cambridge, England: Cambridge University Press, 1995), pp. 1–24. According to Harvey, the term "hermeneutics of suspicion" comes from Paul Ricoeur.

2 D. Stephen Long, "Fetishizing Feuerbach's God: Contextual Theologies as the End of Modernity," unpublished article, p. 13. Long takes the notion of ontotheology from Etienne Gilson, *Being and Some Philosophers*.

3 Harvey, p. 194.

4 Ibid., p. 196.

5 Ibid.

6 Karl Marx, "Theses on Feuerbach," in *Karl Marx and Friedrich Engels on Religion* (Chico, CA: Scholars Press, 1964), p. 71.

7 Karl Marx and Frederick Engels, "The German Ideology," in *Karl Marx and Friedrich Engels on Religion*, p. 75.

8 Alasdair MacIntyre, *Marxism and Christianity* (Notre Dame, IN: University of Notre Dame Press, 1984), p. 103.

9 MacIntyre (*Marxism and Christianity*, p. 117) offers a suggestion on how to view Marxism that we find helpful at this point, namely, "as a doctrine we cannot adhere to because there are truths it cannot accommodate, yet also a doctrine we cannot entirely discard because it embodies truths inseparable from their connection with Marx's general theoretical formulations."

10 Nicholas Lash, *A Matter of Hope: A Theologian's Reflections on the Thought of Karl Marx* (Notre Dame, IN: University of Notre Dame Press, 1982), p. 140. Lash points out that Marx "took over, unexamined [the] identification of Christianity and 'idealism,' with its consequent suppression of the reality of concrete individuals. And he did so, not out of absent-mindedness, but because this identification illuminated certain features of bourgeois society: of a social formation whose 'ideology' was 'idealist.'

11 Neither Feuerbach nor Marx was of course optimistic in the liberal sense; rather, their optimism stems from the influence on their thought of Hegel and his account of history.

12 For a compelling account of this phenomenon, see Mike Budde, *The (Magic) Kingdom of God: Christianity and the Global Culture Industries* (Boulder, CO: Westview Press, 1997), pp. 80, 82, 91–94, 111–115. For an especially whimsical telling of a similar story, see Rodney Clapp, "The Sin of Winnie the Pooh," in *Border Crossings: Christian Trespasses on Popular Culture and Public Affairs* (Grand Rapids, MI: Brazos, 2000), pp. 171–176.

13 Karl Barth, *Church Dogmatics*, vol. 1, pt. 2, translated by G. T. Thompson and Harold Knight (New York: Scribner's, 1956), p. 316.

14 Ibid., pp. 316–317.

15 Robert Jenson, *Systematic Theology*, vol. 1, *The Triune God* (New York: Oxford University Press, 1997), p. 57.

16 Alasdair MacIntyre, *After Virtue* 2nd ed. (Notre Dame, IN: University of Notre Dame Press, 1984), p. 32.

17 Ibid., p. 33.

18 Ibid., p. 23.

19 Ibid., p. 62.

20 Ibid., p. 220.

21 Anthony Giddens, *Modernity and Self-Identity: Self and Society in the Late Modern Age* (Stanford: Stanford University Press, 1991), p. 15.

22 Ibid., pp. 16–21.

23 For a powerful commentary on the ways the Darwinian myth informs and forms modern societies, see Marilynne Robinson, *The Death of Adam: Essays on Modern Thought* (Boston: Houghton Mifflin, 1998), pp. 28–75.

24 Anthony Giddens, *The Consequences of Modernity* (Stanford: Stanford University Press, 1990), pp. 9, 29–36, 79–82.

25 Giddens, *Modernity and Self-Identity*, p. 32, emphasis in original.

26 Ibid., pp. 33–34.

27 Ibid., p. 75.

28 Ibid., p. 71; see p. 76.

29 Ibid., p. 80.

30 Ibid., p. 170.

31 Ibid.

32 Christopher Lasch, *The Culture of Narcissism: American Life in an Age of Diminishing Expectations* (New York: Norton, 1979), p. 5.

33 Gerald McKenny, *To Relieve the Human Condition: Bioethics, Technology and the Body* (Albany: State University of New York Press, 1997), p. 2.

34 Lasch, p. 188.

35 Lasch, p. 92, notes that "advertising encourages men as well as women to see the creation of the self as the highest form of creativity."

36 Ibid., pp. 207–208, quotation at 208.

37 Ibid., pp. 209–211.

38 Ibid., p. 217.

39 Philip Rieff, *The Triumph of the Therapeutic: Uses of Faith after Freud* (Chicago: University of Chicago Press, 1987), p. 13.

40 James Nolan, *The Therapeutic State: Justifying Government at Century's End* (New York: New York University Press, 1998), p. 2. See Lasch, pp. 7–13.

41 Nolan, p. 8.

42 Rieff, p. 29.

43 Ibid., p. 30.

44 Ibid., p. 31.

45 Ibid., p. 48.

46 Ibid., p. 234.

47 Ibid., pp. 239–241, quotation at 241. See Lasch, p. 13.

48 Gary Dorrien, *Soul in Society: The Making and Renewal of Social Christianity* (Minneapolis: Fortress Press, 1995), pp. 217–218.

49 Giddens, *Modernity and Self Identity*, p. 170.

50 Lasch, p. 72.

51 Giddens, *Modernity and Self Identity*, p. 172.

52 Lasch, p. 72.

53 Stephen Crook, Jan Pakulski, and Malcolm Waters, *Postmodernization: Changes in Advanced Society* (London: Sage, 1992), p. 55, quoting Colin Campbell, *The Romantic Ethic and the Spirit of Modern Consumerism* (Oxford: Blackwell, 1987).

54 John Kavanaugh, *Following Christ in a Consumer Society*, 2nd edition (Maryknoll, NY: Orbis, 1991), p. 31.

55 Giddens, *Modernity and Self Identity*, p. 197.

56 Ibid.

57 Nicholas Boyle, *Who Are We Now? Christian Humanism and the Global Market from Hegel to Heaney* (South Bend, IN: University of Notre Dame Press, 1998), p. 27.

58 Ibid., p. 28.

59 Giddens, *Modernity and Self Identity*, p. 197.

60 Georg Lukacs, *History and Class Consciousness: Studies in Marxist Dialectics*, translated by Rodney Livingston (Cambridge: MIT Press, 1971), p. 83.

61 John Milbank, *Theology and Social Theory: Beyond Secular Reason* (Cambridge, MA: Blackwell, 1990), pp. 31–40.

62 John Milbank, "Socialism of the Gift, Socialism by Grace," *New Blackfriars* 77(910), 1996, p. 536.

63 Ibid., p. 535.

64 According to Frederick Jameson, this is the particular characteristic of what is variously called late, postindustrial, or multinational capitalism. He suggests that this is "the purest form of capital yet to have emerged, a prodigious expansion of capital into hitherto uncommodified areas. This purer capitalism of our own time thus eliminates the enclaves of precapitalist organization it had hitherto tolerated and exploited in a tributary way." *Postmodernism, or, the Cultural Logic of Late Capitalism* (Durham, NC: Duke University Press, 1991), p. 36.

65 Ibid., pp. 263–264. Jameson says, rightly, we think, that this "is the proposition

that cannot be allowed to stand unchallenged . . . it is the most crucial terrain of the ideological struggle in our time. If you let it pass because it seems an inconsequential admission or, worse yet, because you've really come to believe in it yourself, in your 'heart of hearts,' then socialism and Marxism alike will have effectively become delegitimated, at least for a time."

66 Ibid., p. 267.

67 Lukacs, p. 91.

68 Lukacs, pp. 92–103, quotation at 93.

69 Karl Barth, *Church Dogmatics*, vol. 3, pt. 4, *The Doctrine of Creation*, edited by G. W. Bromiley and T. F. Torrance (Edinburgh: T. and T. Clark, 1961), pp. 356–357.

70 Ibid., p. 363.

71 Wendell Berry, "Health as Membership," in *Another Turn of the Crank* (Washington, DC: Counterpoint, 1995), p. 90.

72 For an interesting account of the pervasiveness of commodity fetishism in late modernity, see Robert Miklitsch, *From Hegel to Madonna: Towards a General Economy of "Commodity Fetishism"* (Albany: State University of New York Press, 1998), especially pp. 66–67.

73 William C. Placher, *The Domestication of Transcendence: How Modern Thinking about God Went Wrong* (Louisville: Westminster John Knox Press, 1996), pp. 190–197,see especially p. 193.

74 Herbert Benson, *Timeless Healing: The Power and Biology of Belief* (New York: Scribner, 1996) pp. 214–215.

75 Richard Wentz, "The Domestication of the Divine," *Theology Today*, 57(1), April 2000, p. 24.

76 Placher, pp. 71–76; see chapter 2.

77 Placher, p. 75.

78 Wentz, p. 27.

79 Ibid., p. 27.

80 Ibid., p. 27.

81 Ibid., p. 33.

82 Alasdair MacIntyre, *After Virtue*, 2nd ed. (Notre Dame, IN: University of Notre Dame Press, 1984), p. 187.

83 Joseph Dunne, *Back to the Rough Ground: Practical Judgment and the Lure of Technique* (Notre Dame, IN: University of Notre Dame Press, 1993), p. 5.

84 Joseph Dunne says (p. 360): "The compromised state that one finds oneself in, as a historical being, can make the uncompromised position of the technician appear in an attractive light; and the history of technique, and in particular the history of its modern expansion, has been an attempt to overcome history—to create `the peculiar semblance of post-histoire.' This is only a semblance, because, for example, those who promote the behavioral objectives model of teaching are themselves involved in a deeply historical project, whose roots, as this study has tried to show, lie deep in Greek philosophy. Such a project involves a loss of significant substance as the

price to be paid for its gains in rigor and apparent control. But fascination with the gains serves to distract attention from the losses which they entail."

85 For a historical account of the emergence and development of the Christian commitment to the sick, especially as that commitment was institutionalized in hospitals, see Guenter B. Risse, *Mending Bodies, Saving Souls: A History of Hospitals* (New York: Oxford University Press, 1999), pp. 69–165.

86 John Howard Yoder, *The Royal Priesthood: Essays Ecclesiological and Ecumenical* (Grand Rapids, MI: Eerdmans, 1994), p. 74.

Chapter 4

1 Herbert Benson, *Timeless Healing: The Power and Biology of Belief* (New York: Scribner, 1996), p. 197.

2 Ibid., p. 198.

3 J. A. Di Noia, "Religion and the Religions," in *The Cambridge Companion to Karl Barth*, edited by John Webster (Cambridge, England: Cambridge University Press, 2000), p. 244.

4 Karl Barth, *Church Dogmatics,* vol. 1, pt. 2, translated by G. T. Thompson and Harold Knight (New York: Scribner's, 1956), p. 316.

5 Karl Barth, *Church Dogmatics*, vol. 1, pt. 1, translated by G. W. Bromiley (Edinburgh: T. and T. Clark, 1975), p. 3.

6 Di Noia, p. 246.

7 Karl Barth, *Church Dogmatics,* vol. 1, pt. 2, translated by G. T. Thomson and Harold Knight (Edinburgh: T. and T. Clark, 1975), p. 280.

8 Ibid., pp. 280–281, emphasis added.

9 Ibid., p. 281.

10 Ibid., p. 281.

11 Ibid., pp. 281–282.

12 Ibid., p. 297.

13 Ibid., p. 294, see Di Noia, pp. 245–249.

14 Michael Buckley, *At the Origins of Modern Atheism* (New Haven: Yale University Press, 1987).

15 See Kathleen Norris, *The Quotidian Mysteries: Laundry, Liturgy and "Women's Work"* (Mahwah, NJ: Paulist Press, 1998).

16 Nicholas Lash, *The Beginning and the End of "Religion"* (Cambridge, England: Cambridge University Press, 1996), p. 127.

17 Ibid., p. 89.

18 Bruce McCormack, *Karl Barth's Critically Realistic Dialectical Theology: Its Genesis and Development, 1909–1936* (Oxford: Clarendon Press, 1995), p. 247.

19 Nicholas Lash, *A Matter of Hope: A Theologian's Reflections on the Thought of Karl Marx* (Notre Dame, IN: University of Notre Dame Press, 1981), pp. 135–152.

20 Ibid., p. 144.

21 Ibid.

22 John Milbank, *Theology and Social Theory: Beyond Secular Reason* (Cambridge, MA: Blackwell, 1990), pp. 208–209.

23 Ibid., p. 381.

24 Ibid., pp. 385–386.

25 For helpful accounts of performance and the biblical narrative, see, for example, Richard Hays, *Echoes of Scripture in the Letters of Paul* (New Haven: Yale University Press, 1989), and N. T. Wright, *The New Testament and the People of God* (Minneapolis: Fortress Press, 1992).

26 Barth, *Church Dogmatics,* vol. 1, pt. 1, pp. 136, 137.

27 Ibid., p. 138.

28 Barth, *Church Dogmatics,* vol. 1, pt. 2, p. 41.

29 Ibid., p. 43.

30 Karl Barth, *The Humanity of God* (Louisville: John Knox Press, 1960), p. 46, emphasis in original.

31 Barth, *Church Dogmatics,* vol. 1, pt. 2, p. 346.

32 Ibid.

33 Milbank, pp. 217–223.

34 Robert Jenson, *Systematic Theology,* vol. 2, *The Works of God* (Oxford: Oxford University Press, 1999), p. 318.

35 Ibid., p. 314.

36 McCormack, p. 255.

37 Karl Barth, *The Epistle to the Romans*, translated from the 6th ed. by Edwyn C. Hoskins (London: Oxford University Press, 1968), p. 97.

38 Hebrews 2:10b, 4:15b, NRSV.

39 John Howard Yoder, *The Politics of Jesus* (Grand Rapids, MI: Eerdmans, 1972), pp. 115–134.

40 Lash, p. 243.

41 Barth, *Church Dogmatics*, vol. 3, pt. 4, 324, distinguishes this Christian respect for life from the view of Albert Schweitzer, which is the view that life is "the supreme good." Barth says, "life for us cannot be a supreme principle at all, although it can be a sphere in relation to which ethics has to investigate the content and consequences of God's command. That life should be accepted, treated and preserved with respect is for the moment, however, a suitable formulation of the answer we must give in this field from the first if not from every standpoint." See pp. 334–335.

42 Ibid., p. 340.

43 Ibid., p. 340.

44 Ibid., p. 343.

45 Ibid., p. 344.

46 Wendell Berry, *What Are People For?* (New York: North Point Press, 1990), p. 9.

47 Barth, *Church Dogmatics*, vol. 3, pt. 4. p. 327.

48 Ibid., p. 341.

49 Ibid., p. 357.

50 Ibid., pp. 357–358.

51 Alasdair MacIntyre, *Dependent Rational Animals; Why Human Beings Need the Virtues* (Chicago: Open Court, 1999), p. 73.

52 Barth, *Church Dogmatics*, vol. 3, pt. 4, p. 366.

53 John 9:1–41, quotations from vv. 2–3.

54 James Alison, *The Joy of Being Wrong: Original Sin through Easter Eyes* (New York: Crossroad, 1998), p. 120.

55 Barth, *Church Dogmatics*, vol. 3, pt. 4, pp. 366–367.

56 In chapter 5 we attempt to concretely specify some of these ways Christians are called to struggle against illness.

57 Saint Basil the Great, "The Long Rules" in *Saint Basil Ascetical Works*, translated by Monica Wagner (Washington, DC: Catholic University of America Press, 1962), p. 331. Cited in H. Tristam Engelhardt, "Genetic Enhancement and Theosis: Two Models of Therapy," *Christian Bioethics* 5(2), 1999, pp. 197–199.

58 Barth, *Church Dogmatics*, vol. 3, pt. 4, p. 370.

59 Ibid., p. 371.

60 Ibid., pp. 588–589.

61 Ibid., p. 342.

62 Ibid., p. 374.

63 Ibid.

64 David Toole, *Waiting for Godot in Sarajevo: Theological Reflections on Nihilism, Tragedy, and Apocalypse* (Boulder, CO: Westview Press, 1998).

65 John Howard Yoder, *The Politics of Jesus*, 2nd ed. (Grand Rapids, MI: Eerdmans, 1998), p. 245. See Toole, p. 209.

66 Toole, p. 210, says: "To adopt an apocalyptic style is to follow the biblical lead and turn our attention away from the power of kings and toward the power of ravens and peasant prophets in the wilderness."

67 John Howard Yoder, "Ethics and Eschatology," in *Ex Auditu* 6, 1990, p. 119.

68 Ibid., p. 120; see Toole, p. 211.

69 Isaiah 43:1b–2, NRSV.

70 John Howard Yoder, *The Politics of Jesus*, 1st ed. (Grand Rapids, MI: Eerdmans, 1972), p. 238. Unless otherwise noted, all references to this work hereafter are from the first edition.

71 Toole, p. 215.

72 Ibid., p. 216.

73 Yoder, *Politics of Jesus*, p. 238.

74 Toole, p. 222.

75 Yoder, *Politics of Jesus*, p. 132.

76 Wendell Berry, "Health as Membership," in *Another Turn of the Crank* (Washington, DC: Counterpoint, 1995), p. 94.

77 *Politics of Jesus*, p. 132.

78 For a further development of this point, see Stanley Hauerwas, *Naming the Silences: God, Medicine and the Problem of Suffering* (Grand Rapids, MI: Eerd-

mans, 1991). Also see Joel Shuman, *The Body of Compassion: Ethics, Medicine and the Church* (Boulder, CO: Westview Press, 1999).

79 Hauerwas, p. 34.

80 Yoder, "Ethics and Eschatology," p. 123.

81 *Politics of Jesus*, p. 238.

82 Alison, p. 76.

83 Barth, *Humanity of God*, p. 62.

Chapter 5

1 Hayden Carruth, "Crucifixion," from *Collected Shorter Poems 1946–1991* (Port Townsend, WA: Copper Canyon Press, 1992), p. 412.

2 A central biblical text in this regard is James 5:14–16: "Are any among you sick? They should call the elders of the church and have them pray over them, anointing them with oil in the name of the Lord. The prayer of faith will save the sick, and the Lord will lift them up; and anyone who has committed any sins will be forgiven. Therefore confess your sins to one another, and pray for one another, so that you may be healed. The prayer of the righteous is powerful and effective." For an overview of the ways this text has been understood and ritually practiced in the several strands of the Christian tradition, see Karen Westerfield Tucker, "Christian Rituals Surrounding Sickness," in *Life Cycles in Jewish and Christian Worship*, edited by Paul Bradshaw and Lawrence Hoffman, (Notre Dame, IN: University of Notre Dame Press, 1996), pp. 154–172.

3 Revelation 5:6, NRSV.

4 Donald Hall, *Without* (Boston: Mariner Books, 1998), p. 13.

5 Ibid., p. 17.

6 Michael Blumenthal, "And the Wages of Goodness Are Not Assured," in *The Wages of Goodness* (Columbia: University of Missouri Press, 1992), p. 54.

7 Thomas Aquinas, *Summa Theologica*, 2a–2ae q. 15, art. 1.2, from the complete English edition in five volumes, translated by the Fathers of the English Dominican Province (Allen, TX: Christian Classics, 1981), pp. 1236–1237.

8 Wendell Berry, *A Place on Earth* (Revision) (New York: North Point Press, 1983), pp. 8–9.

9 Ibid., pp. 94–95.

10 Ibid., p. 231.

11 Ibid., pp. 257–258.

12 Adolf von Harack, "Medicinishes aus der altesten Kirkengeschichte," in *Texte Untersuchungen zur Geschichte der alterchristlichen Literatur* (Leipzig: J. C. Hinrich, 1892), vol. 8, pt. 4, pp. 37–152, quoted in Gary Ferngren, "Early Christianity as a Religion of Healing," *Bulletin of the History of Medicine* 66, 1992, p. 1.

13 Ferngren, pp. 2–3.

14 Ibid., p. 3.

15 Here see Stanley Hauerwas, *The Peaceable Kingdom: A Primer in Christian*

Ethics (Notre Dame, IN: University of Notre Dame Press, 1983), pp. 72–95.

16 For a remarkable development of the theology behind this claim, see Douglas Farrow, *Ascension and Ecclesia: On the Significance of the Doctrine of the Ascension for Ecclesiology and Christian Cosmology* (Grand Rapids, MI: Eerdmans, 1999).

17 Ferngren, p. 14, says that it is a mistake to "speak of the care of the sick as a special 'healing ministry' of the early church. It was an important part, but only a part, of the general philanthropic outreach of the church, which included caring for widows and orphans, aiding the poor, visiting those in prison, and extending hospitality to travelers. . . . The theme of Christus Medicus (Jesus the Great Physician) was indeed a prominent one in the early church. But the phrase was used metaphorically to refer to Jesus as the healer primarily of the afflictions of the soul, and only rarely of the diseases of the body."

18 Hector Avalos, *Health Care and the Rise of Christianity* (Peabody, MA: Hendrickson, 1999), p. 19.

19 Guenter B. Risse, *Mending Bodies, Saving Souls: A History of Hospitals* (New York: Oxford University Press, 1999), p. 73.

20 Ibid., pp. 72; 87–94.

21 Ibid., pp. 73–74.

22 See Joel Shuman, *The Body of Compassion: Ethics, Medicine and the Church* (Boulder, CO: Westview Press, 1999), especially chapter 4.

23 James Alison, *The Joy of Being Wrong: Original Sin through Easter Eyes* (New York: Crossroad Herder, 1998), p. 120. Our argument about the significance of this story closely follows Alison.

24 Ibid., p. 120.

25 Ibid., p. 121.

26 Ibid., p. 121.

27 Ibid., p. 125.

28 John Zizioulas, *Being as Communion: Studies in Personhood and the Church* (Crestwood, NY: St. Vladimir's Seminary Press, 1993), p. 17.

29 Ibid., p. 19.

30 John Milbank, *Theology and Social Theory: Beyond Secular Reason* (Oxford: Blackwell, 1990), p. 232.

31 Ibid., p. 236; see Zizioulas, p. 46.

32 Robert Jenson, *Systematic Theology,* vol. 2, *The Works of God* (New York: Oxford University Press, 1999), p. 25.

33 Ibid., p. 25.

34 Ibid, p. 35.

35 Jenson says (p. 45): "We will then say: to be a creature is, in christological respect, to be a revelation of God's will. In a more dramatic and therefore more accurate language we found in Luther, to be a creature is to be a 'created word' from God."

36 Ibid., p. 76.

37 See Zizioulas, pp. 151–152.

38 We are indebted here to David Toole, *Waiting for Godot in Sarajevo: Theological Reflections on Nihilism, Tragedy and Apocalypse* (Boulder, CO: Westview Press, 1998), pp. 227–241.

39 Here we find the work of Paul Waddell especially helpful. See his *Friendship and the Moral Life* (Notre Dame, IN: University of Notre Dame Press, 1989).

40 Thomas Aquinas, *Summa Theologica*, 2a–2ae, q. 30, art. 1; see Alasdair MacIntyre, *Dependent Rational Animals: Why Human Beings Need the Virtues*, (Chicago: Open Court, 1999), pp. 123–124.

41 Waddell, p. 120, quoting Aquinas, *Summa Theologica* 1a–2ae, q. 65, art. 5.

42 Here we disagree with MacIntyre, who suggests that misericordia is a virtue necessary to all human community and so not a species of the theological virtue of charity. While it is certainly true that all human communities require something like misericordia, we believe that a full account of the virtue requires an account of the virtue of charity from which it flows. Even among those who do not identify their concern for others as flowing from God's charity, such concern is always dependent on that grace of God that is present to and sustains all of creation. Thanks to Stanley Hauerwas for pointing this out to us.

43 *Dependent Rational Animals*, p. 125.

44 Aquinas, *Summa Thelogicau*, 2a–2ae, q. 30, art. 2.

45 Ibid., emphasis added. See MacIntyre, *Dependent Rational Animals*, p. 125.

46 *Dependent Rational Animals*, pp. 126–127.

47 Ibid., p. 128.

48 Ibid., pp. 138–139.

49 Ibid., pp. 138–139.

50 Ibid., p. 145.

51 Wendell Berry, "Fidelity," in *Fidelity: Five Stories* (New York: Pantheon, 1992), p. 107.

52 Ibid., p. 108.

53 Ibid., p. 110.

54 Ibid., p. 113.

55 Ibid., p. 160.

56 Ibid., p. 133.

57 Ibid., p. 169.

58 Ibid., p. 189.

Bibliography

Alison, James. *The Joy of Being Wrong: Original Sin through Easter Eyes*. New York: Crossroad Herder, 1998.

Aquinas, Thomas. *Summa Theologica*. Translated by the Fathers of the English Dominican Province. Allen, TX: Christian Classics, 1981.

Augustine. *Confessions*. Translated by R. S. Pine-Coffin. New York: Penguin, 1961.

Augustine. *On Christian Doctrine*. Translated by D. W. Robertson, Jr. Upper Saddle River, NJ: Prentice Hall, 1958.

Augustine. *The Catholic and Manichaean Ways of Life*. Translated by Donald A. Gallagher and Idella J. Gallagher. Washington, D.C.: Catholic University of America Press, 1966.

Avalos, Hector. *Health Care and the Rise of Christianity*. Peabody, MA: Hendrickson, 1999.

Barth, Karl. *Church Dogmatics*, Vol. 1. Pt. 1. Translated by G. W. Bromiley. Edinburgh: T. and T. Clark, 1975.

Barth, Karl. *Church Dogmatics*, Vol. 1. Pt. 2. Translated by G. T. Thompson and Harold Knight. Edinburgh: T. and T. Clark, 1975.

Barth, Karl. *Church Dogmatics*. Vol. 1, Pt. 2. Translated by G. T. Thompson and Harold Knight. New York: Scribner's, 1956.

Barth, Karl. *Church Dogmatics*, Vol. 3, Pt. 4. *The Doctrine of Creation*. Edited by G. W. Bromiley and T. F. Torrance. Edinburgh: T. and T. Clark, 1961.

Barth, Karl. *The Epistle to the Romans*. Translated by Edwyn C. Hoskins. London: Oxford University Press, 1968.

Barth, Karl. *The Humanity of God*. Louisville: John Knox Press, 1960.

Beauchamp, Dan. *The Health of the Republic*. Philadelphia: Temple University Press, 1988.

Benson, Herbert. *Beyond the Relaxation Response*. New York: Berkley Books, 1985.

Benson, Herbert. "The Nocebo Effect: History and Physiology." *Preventive Medicine* 26 (1997): 612.

Benson, Herbert. *Timeless Healing: The Power of Biology and Belief*. New York: Scribner, 1996.

Berry, Wendell. *Fidelity: Five Stories*. New York: Pantheon, 1992.

Berry, Wendell. "Health as Membership." In *Another Turn of the Crank*. Washington DC, Counterpoint, 1995.

Berry, Wendell. *A Place on Earth* (Revision). New York: North Point Press, 1983.

Berry, Wendell. *What Are People For?* New York: North Point Press, 1990.

Bloom, Harold. *The American Religion: The Emergence of the Post-Christian Nation.* New York: Simon and Schuster, 1992.

Blumenthal, Michael. *The Wages of Goodness.* Columbia: University of Missouri Press, 1992.

Boyle, Nicholas. *Who Are We Now? Christian Humanism and the Global Market from Hegel to Heaney.* South Bend, IN: University of Notre Dame Press, 1998.

Browder, David. "Elected Suffering: Toward a Theology for Medicine." Ph.D. diss. Duke University, 1991.

Buckley, Michael. *At the Origins of Modern Atheism.* New Haven: Yale University Press, 1987.

Budde, Mike. *The (Magic) Kingdom of God: Christianity and the Global Culture Industries.* Boulder, CO: Westview Press, 1997.

Burt, Donald. *Friendship and Society: An Introduction to Augustine's Practical Philosophy.* Grand Rapids, MI: Eerdmans, 1999.

Bynum, W. F., and Roy Porter. *The Companion Encyclopedia of the History of Medicine.* New York: Routledge, 1993.

Callahan, Daniel. "Death and the Research Imperative." *New England Journal of Medicine* 342(9) (2000): 654.

Campbell, Colin. *The Romantic Ethic and the Spirit of Modern Consumerism.* Oxford: Blackwell, 1987.

Carruth, Hayden. *Collected Shorter Poems 1946–1991.* Port Townsend, WA: Copper Canyon Press, 1992.

Clapp, Rodney. *Border Crossings: Christian Trespasses on Popular Culture and Public Affairs.* Grand Rapids, MI: Brazos, 2000.

Copleston, Frederick. *A History of Philosophy.* New York: Doubleday, 1965.

Crook, Stephen, Jan Pakulski, and Malcolm Waters. *Postmodernization: Change in Advanced Society.* London: Sage, 1992.

Dalferth, Ingolf. "'I Determine What God Is!' Theology in the Age of 'Cafeteria Religion.'" *Theology Today* 57(1) (2000): 5–23.

Danis, Marion, et al. "Incorporating Palliative Care into Critical Care Education: Principles, Challenges, and Opportunities." *Critical Care Medicine* 27(9) (1999): 2005–2013.

Di Noia, J. A. "Religion and the Religious." In *The Cambridge Companion to Karl Barth,* edited by John Webster. Cambridge, England: Cambridge University Press, 2000.

Dorrien, Gary. *Soul in Society: The Making and Renewal of Social Christianity.* Minneapolis: Fortress Press, 1995.

Dossey, Larry. "Do Religion and Spirituality Matter in Health? A Response to the Recent Article in *The Lancet.*" *Alternative Therapies* 5(3) (1999): 16–18.

Dossey, Larry. *Healing Words.* San Francisco: Harper, 1993.

Dossey, Larry. *Prayer Is Good Medicine.* San Francisco: Harper, 1996.

Dossey, Larry. *Reinventing Medicine.* San Francisco: Harper, 1999.

Dreyfus, Herbert, and Paul Rabinow, eds. *Michel Foucault: Beyond Structuralism and Hermeneutics.* Chicago: University of Chicago Press, 1982.

Dunne, Joseph. *Back to the Rough Ground: Practical Judgment and the Lure of Technique.* Notre Dame, IN: University of Notre Dame Press, 1993.

Dwyer, Jeffrey, et al. "The Effects of Religious Concentration and Affiliation on County Cancer Mortality Rates." *Journal of Health and Social Behavior* 31 (1990): 189.

Ellison, C. G., and J. S. Levin. "The Religion-Health Connection: Evidence, Theory, and Future Directions." *Health Education and Behavior* 25(6) (1998): 700–720.

Englehardt, H. Tristam. "Genetic Enhancement and Theosis: Two Models of Therapy." *Christian Bioethics* 5(2) (1999): 197–199.

Ewing, A. C. *A Short Commentary on Kant's Critique of Pure Reason.* Chicago: University of Chicago Press, 1938.

Farrow, Douglas. *Ascension and Ecclesia: On the Significance of the Doctrine of the Ascension for Ecclesiology and Christian Cosmology.* Grand Rapids, MI: Eerdmans, 1999.

Ferngren, Gary. "Early Christianity as a Religion of Healing." *Bulletin of the History of Medicine* 66 (1992): 1.

Feuerbach, Ludwig. *The Essence of Christianity.* Translated by George Eliot. New York: Harper, 1957.

Feuerbach, Ludwig. *Lectures on the Essence of Religion.* Translated by Ralph Manheim. New York: Harper and Row, 1967.

Foucault, Michel. *Discipline and Punish.* New York: Vintage, 1979.

Foucault, Michel. *The History of Sexuality.* Translated by Robert Hurley. New York: Random House, 1978.

Foucault, Michel. *The Order of Things: An Archaeology of the Human Sciences.* New York: Vintage Books, 1973.

Foucault, Michel. *Power/Knowledge.* Edited by Colin Gordon. Translated by Coin Gordon et al. New York: Pantheon, 1980.

Frank, Arthur. *At the Will of the Body.* Boston: Houghton Mifflin, 1991.

Frei, Hans. *The Eclipse of Biblical Narrative.* New Haven: Yale University Press, 1974.

Giddens, Anthony. *The Consequences of Modernity.* Stanford: Stanford University Press, 1990.

Giddens, Anthony. *Modernity and Self-Identity: Self and Society in the Late Modern Age.* Stanford: Stanford University Press, 1991.

Haggard, Howard. *Mystery, Magic and Medicine: The Rise of Medicine from Superstition to Science.* Garden City, NY: Doubleday and Doran, 1933.

Hall, Donald. *Without.* Boston: Mariner Books, 1998.

Harvey, Van. *Feuerbach and the Interpretation of Religion.* Cambridge, England: Cambridge University Press, 1995.

Hauerwas, Stanley. *Naming the Silences: God, Medicine and the Problem of Suffering.* Grand Rapids, MI: Eerdmans, 1990.

Hauerwas, Stanley. *The Peaceable Kingdom: A Primer in Christian Ethics.* Notre Dame, IN: University of Notre Dame Press, 1983.

Haug, Marie, and Bebe Levin. *Consumerism in Medicine.* Beverly Hills: Sage, 1983.

Hays, Richard. *Echoes of Scripture in the Letters of Paul.* New Haven: Yale University Press, 1989.

Illich, Ivan. *Medical Nemesis: The Expropriation of Health.* New York: Pantheon, 1976.

Jameson, Frederic. *Postmodernism, or, the Cultural Logic of Late Capitalism.* Durham, NC: Duke University Press, 1991.

Jenson, Robert. "How the World Lost Its Story." *First Things* October (1993): 19–24.

Jenson, Robert. *Systematic Theology,* Vol. 1, *The Triune God.* New York: Oxford University Press, 1997.

Jenson, Robert. *Systematic Theology,* Vol. 2, *The Works of God.* New York: Oxford University Press, 1999.

Jones, L. Gregory. *Transformed Judgment.* Notre Dame, IN: University of Notre Dame Press, 1990.

Kant, Immanuel. *Religion within the Limits of Reason Alone.* New York: Harper and Row, 1960.

Kavanaugh, John. *Following Christ in a Consumer Society.* 2nd ed. Maryknoll, NY: Orbis, 1991.

Kenneson, Phil, and James Street. *Selling Out the Church.* Nashville: Abingdon Press, 1997.

King, D. E., and B. Bushwick. "Beliefs and Attitudes of Hospital Inpatients about Faith Healing and Prayer." *Journal of Family Practice* 39(4) (1994): 349–352.

King, Lester. *The Growth of Medical Thought.* Chicago: University of Chicago Press, 1963.

Kleinman, Arthur. *The Illness Narratives.* New York: Basic Books, 1981.

Koenig, Harold. *The Healing Power of Faith.* New York: Simon and Schuster, 1999.

Koenig, Harold. *Is Religion Good for Your Health?* New York: Haworth Pastoral Press, 1999.

Koenig, Harold, and David Larson. "Use of Hospital Services, Religious Attendance, and Religious Affiliation." *Southern Medical Journal* 91(10) (1998): 925–932.

Koenig, Harold, et al. "Religion, Spirituality, and Medicine: A Rebuttal to Skeptics." *International Journal of Psychiatry in Medicine* 29(2) (1999): 123–131.

Koenig, Harold, et al. "Attendance at Religious Services, Interleukin-6, and Other Biological Parameters of Immune Function in Older Adults." *International Journal of Psychiatry in Medicine* 27(3) (1997): 233–250.

Koenig, Harold, et al. "The Relationship between Religious Activities and Blood Pressure in Older Adults." *International Journal of Psychiatry in Medicine* 28(2) (1998): 189–213.

Lasch, Christopher. *The Culture of Narcissism: American Life in an Age of Diminishing Expectations.* New York: Norton, 1979.

Lasch, Christopher. *The True and Only Heaven.* New York: Norton, 1991.

Lash, Nicholas. *The Beginning and the End of "Religion."* Cambridge, England: Cambridge University Press, 1996.

Lash, Nicholas. *A Matter of Hope: A Theologian's Reflections on the Thought of Karl Marx.* Notre Dame, IN: University of Notre Dame Press, 1981.

Levin, Jeffrey. "How Religion Influences Morbidity and Health: Reflections on Natural History, Salutogenesis and Host Resistance." *Social Science and Medicine* 43(5) (1996): 849–864.

Levin, Jeffrey. "Religion and Health: Is There an Association, Is It Valid, and Is It Causal?" *Social Science and Medicine* 38(11) (1994): 1475–1482.

Lindbeck, George. *The Nature of Doctrine.* Philadelphia: Westminster Press, 1984.

Lo, Bernard, et al. "Discussing Palliative Care with Patients." *Annals of Internal Medicine* 130(9) (1999): 744–749.

Long, D. Stephen. "Fetishizing Feuerbach's God: Contextual Theologies as the End of Modernity." Unpublished article.

Lukacs, Georg. *History and Class Consciousness: Studies in Marxist Dialectics.* Translated by Rodney Livingston. Cambridge: MIT Press, 1971.

MacIntyre, Alasdair. *After Virtue.* 2nd ed. Notre Dame, IN: University of Notre Dame Press, 1984.

MacIntyre, Alasdair. *Dependent Rational Animals; Why Human Beings Need the Virtues.* Chicago: Open Court, 1999.

MacIntyre, Alasdair. *Marxism and Christianity.* Notre Dame, IN: University of Notre Dame Press, 1984.

MacIntyre, Alasdair. "Patients as Agents." In *Philosophical Medical Ethics: Its Nature and Significance,* edited by . Eds. S. F. Spicker and H. T. Engelhardt. Dordrecht: D. Reidel, 1977.

MacIntyre, Alasdair. *Three Rival Versions of Moral Enquiry.* Notre Dame, IN: University of Notre Dame Press, 1990.

Marx, Karl. "Theses on Feuerbach." *Karl Marx and Friedrich Engels on Religion.* Chico, CA: Scholars Press, 1964.

Marx, Karl, and Frederick Engels. "The German Ideology." *Karl Marx and Friedrich Engels on Religion.* Chico, CA: Scholars Press, 1964.

Matthews, Dale. *The Faith Factor: Proof of the Healing Power of Prayer.* New York: Penguin Books, 1998.

Matthews, Dale, David Larson, and Constance Berry. *The Faith Factor: An Annotated Bibliography of Clinical Research on Spiritual Subjects.* Rockville, MD: National Institute for Healthcare Research, 1993.

Matthews, Dale, et al. "Religious Commitment and Health Status: A Review of the Research and Implications for Family Medicine." *Archives of Family Medicine* 8(6) (1999): 476.

McCormack, Bruce. *Karl Barth's Critically Realistic Dialectical Theology: Its Genesis and Development, 1909–1936.* Oxford: Clarendon Press, 1995.

McKenny, Gerald. *To Relieve the Human Condition: Bioethics, Technology and the Body.* Albany: State University of New York Press, 1997.

Meador, K. G., and S. C. Henson. "Growing Old in a Therapeutic Culture." *Theology Today* 57(2) (2000): 185–202.

Milbank, John. "Socialism of the Gift, Socialism by Grace." *New Blackfriars* 77(910) (1996), 532–547.

Milbank, John. *Theology and Social Theory: Beyond Secular Reason.* Oxford: Blackwell, 1990.

Miklitsch, Robert. *From Hegel to Madonna: Towards a General Economy of "Commodity Fetishism."* Albany: State University of New York Press, 1998.

Nolan, James. *The Therapeutic State: Justifying Government at Century's End.* New York: New York University Press, 1998.

Norris, Kathleen. *The Quotidian Mysteries: Laundry, Liturgy and "Women's Work."* Mahwah, NJ: Paulist Press, 1998.

Null and, Sherwin. *Doctors: The Biography of Medicine.* New York: Vintage Books, 1988.

Pakulski, Jan, and Malcolm Waters. *Postmodernization: Change in Advanced Society.* London: Sage, 1992.

Pellegrino, Edmund, and David Thomasma. *A Philosophical Basis of Medical Practice.* New York: Oxford University Press, 1981.

Placher, William C. *The Domestication of Transcendence: How Modern Thinking about God Went Wrong.* Louisville: Westminster John Knox Press, 1996.

Rawls, John. *Political Liberalism.* New York: Columbia University Press, 1993.

Rieff, Philip. *The Triumph of the Therapeutic: Uses of Faith After Freud.* Chicago: University of Chicago Press, 1987.

Risse, Geunter B. *Mending Bodies, Saving Souls: A History of Hospitals.* New York: Oxford University Press, 1999.

Robinson, Marilynne. "Facing Reality." In *The Death of Adam: Essays on Modern Thought.* Boston: Houghton Mifflin, 1998.

Rogers, Eugene. *Thomas Aquinas and Karl Barth: Sacred Doctrine and the Natural Knowledge of God.* Notre Dame, IN: University of Notre Dame Press, 1995.

Rothman, David. "A Century of Failure: Class Barriers to Reform." In *The Politics of Health Care Reform,* edited by James Morone and Gary Belkin. Durham, NC: Duke University Press, 1994.

Schleiermacher, Friedrich. *On Religion: Speeches to Its Cultured Despisers.* Translated by John Oman. New York: Harper, 1958.

Schleiermacher, Friedrich. *The Christian Faith.* English translation of the 2nd German edition. Edited by H. Mackintosh and J. Stewart. Edinburgh: T. and T. Clark, 1989.

Sevensky, Robert. "The Religious Foundations of Health Care: A Conceptual Approach." *Journal of Medical Ethics* 9 (3)(1983):165.

Shuman, Joel. *The Body of Compassion: Ethics, Medicine and the Church.* Boulder, CO: Westview Press, 1999.

Shuman, Joel. "Desperately Seeking Perfection: Christian Discipleship and Medical Genetics." *Christian Bioethics* 5(2) (2000): 139–153.

Sigerist, Henry. *The Great Doctors.* Garden City, NY: Doubleday, 1958.

Sloan, R. P., et al. Editorial. *New England Journal of Medicine* 342(25) (2000): 1913–1916.

Sloan, R. P., et al. "Religion, Spirituality and Medicine." *Lancet* 353 (1999): 664–667.

Taylor, Charles. "Philosophical Reflections on Caring Practices." In *The Crisis of Care,* edited by Susan Phillips and Patricia Benner. Washington, DC: Georgetown University Press, 1994.

Toole, David. *Waiting for Godot in Sarajevo: Theological Reflections on Nihilism, Tragedy and Apocalypse.* Boulder, CO: Westview Press, 1998.

Tucker, Karen Westerfield. "Christian Rituals Surrounding Sickness." In *Life Cycles in Jewish and Christian Worship,* edited by Paul Bradshaw and Lawrence Hoffman. Notre Dame, IN: University of Notre Dame Press, 1996.

Turner, Denys. *Marxism and Christianity.* Totowa, NJ: Barnes and Noble, 1983.

Waddell, Paul. *Friendship and the Moral Life.* Notre Dame, IN: University of Notre Dame Press, 1989.

Walzer, Michael. *Spheres of Justice.* New York: Basic Books, 1983.

Wentz, Richard. "The Domestication of the Divine." *Theology Today* 57(1). (April 2000): 24.

Rowan Williams, *Lost Icons: Reflections on Cultural Bereavement* (Edinburgh: T and T Clark, 2000), p. 23.

Wright, N. T. *The New Testament and the People of God.* Minneapolis: Fortress Press, 1992.

Yoder, John Howard. "Ethics and Eschatology." *Ex Auditu* 6 (1990): 119.

Yoder, John Howard. *The Politics of Jesus.* Grand Rapids, MI: Eerdmans, 1972.

Yoder, John Howard. *The Politics of Jesus.* 2nd ed. Grand Rapids, MI: Eerdmans, 1989.

Yoder, John Howard. *The Royal Priesthood: Essays Ecclesiological and Ecumenical.* Grand Rapids, MI: Eerdmans, 1994.

Zizioulas, John. *Being as Communion: Studies in Personhood and the Church.* Crestwood, NY: St. Vladimir's Seminary Press, 1993.

Index

self-revelation as triune society,
127–28
speech of, 100–101
triumph over evil, 111–12
as uncontrollable, 116–18
as "unnecessary," 55–56
Yoder on, 92, 110
grace, 118, 123
great reversal, 41

Hall, Donald, 117
happiness, 68, 86–88
Harnack, Adolf von, 123–24, 125
Harvey, Van, 66, 72, 73
healing, 123–33
Healing Power of Faith, The (Koenig),
34
health
as among most basic of goods, 116
Barth on, 87, 105
in Christian life, 12–14
as commodity, 86–88
as complex, 12
and culture, 9–11
and faith, 21, 35
as fetishized, 6, 88
longing for, 5, 7, 12–13, 95, 102–3
and religion, 15–16, 20–43, 45
and well-lived life, 14–18
See also illness; medicine
hedonism, 10
Hegel, Georg, 65
Hegelians, 65
high capitalism, 82–86
history, 65, 99
holism, 87
hope, 118–23
hospitality, 91–92, 126, 130
human body, 28
human essence, 74
Hutterites, 23

idolatry, 21, 42, 95, 96, 98, 99, 104,
107–8

illness
apocalyptic struggle against, 109–14
Christian politics of, 115–35
Christian struggle against, 107–9,
129–30
Christian traditions regarding, 6–7,
43, 91, 100
hatred of, 3–4
and sin, 105–7, 113, 126
and well-lived life, 14–18
will to be free of, 105
See also health; medicine
imagination, 99
immune system, 23
inclusion, 129
individualism, 10, 73, 75, 76–77, 84–85,
86
industrialism, 76
institutions, 76–77
integrity, 77
internally referential line of development, 77
intuition of the infinite, 59–60
Isaiah (prophet), 111
isolation, 76, 77

James, William, 71
Jenson, Robert, 19, 75
Jesus of Nazareth, 98, 99, 100, 108
apocalyptic style, 111
Bloom on, 8
and Christian longing, 4
conflict against sickness, 107
cross of, 102, 111, 112–13, 116
and friendship with God, 15
and God's speech, 101
healing acts, 124, 125, 126–27
Hegel on, 65
particularity to Christianity, 101–2
and relation between suffering and
sin, 106
resurrection, 69–70, 102, 111,
113–14, 126
as sinner, 103